Butterfly Island

It seemed to Vo Diem that he'd been running all his life, but he kept going, driven by anger as well as fear.

Diem paused at the airport access road, gasping for breath. Too busy to be safe, he looked for another, more secure route.

The lives of a young Vietnamese on the run and a family of Australians, fighting to keep their home, Butterfly Island, on the Great Barrier Reef, become unintentionally and irrevocably entwined in this exciting novel, based on the BBC television drama series, *Butterfly Island*.

This story is based on the television series *Butterfly Island* first shown on BBC1 in 1986. The film was made on location in Queensland, Australia by Independent Productions, produced by Brendon Lunney and directed by Frank Arnold. The main characters were played as follows: Charlie Wilson, Grigor Taylor; Sally Wilson, Kerri Sackville; Greg Wilson, Mark Kounnas; Jackie Wilson, Mouche Phillips; Vo Diem, Phu An Chiem; Bob Gallio, Gerry Sont.

Butterfly Island

Rick Searle

Based on the screenplay
by David Phillips

BBC/KNIGHT BOOKS.

for Bronwyn

Copyright © Graphic Descriptions 1986
Television series created by Rick Searle
First published 1986 by British Broadcasting
Corporation/Knight Books
Second impression 1986

British Library C.I.P.

Searle, Rick
    Butterfly Island.
    I. Title
    823′.914[F]   PR6069.E1/

    ISBN 0-340-39458-7

Printed and bound in Great Britain for the British
Broadcasting Corporation, 35 Marylebone High Street,
London W1M 4AA and Hodder and Stoughton
Paperbacks, a division of Hodder and Stoughton Ltd.,
Mill Road, Dunton Green, Sevenoaks, Kent (Editorial
Office: 47 Bedford Square, London WC1B 3DP) by
Richard Clay Ltd., Bungay, Suffolk

FACT OR FICTION?

Butterfly Island is a story, but there are islands just like it in Australia's Great Barrier Reef – one of the wonders of the natural world. It's a vast complex of coral reefs and sandy banks stretching from Anchor Cay, near Cape York, to Lady Elliot Island, two thousand kilometres further south, off the Central Queensland coast. It represents some 10,000 years of coral growth and covers an area about the size of the United Kingdom. This colossal structure has microscopic beginnings, because the architect and engineer of the Reef is the coral polyp, one of the smallest and simplest creatures in the animal kingdom. Polyps thrive off the Queensland coast, their larvae drifting in millions through the warm, shallow, pollution-free seas until they come into contact with a firm surface, where they attach themselves and change. Each polyp constructs a tough, tiny limestone shelter around itself, and there it stays, its miniature tentacles waving in the currents, attracting and gathering food. When eventually the polyp dies, the hard receptacle where it lived remains, providing a firm foundation where other larvae can lodge and build. In this way, millimetre by millimetre, layer by layer, generation by generation the Reef has grown into gargantuan proportions unequalled anywhere else in the world.

The Great Barrier Reef is aptly named, because its coral ramparts protect the coast of Queensland from the full force of the Pacific rollers. On the leeward side the waters are calm, and dotted with idyllic islands which attract tourists from all over the world. As well as the myriad shapes and hues of the corals themselves, they come to see other forms of underwater life that have evolved in, on and around the Reef: brilliantly-coloured fish, turtles, sea birds, exotic shells. They can see it all from glass-bottomed boats and underwater observatories, and still be back in their air-conditioned hotels in time for dinner, without getting their feet wet!

All the characters are invented, but refugees like Vo Diem could easily have found their way to Queensland. In the middle of the nineteen-seventies, when war had devastated their country, thousands of Vietnamese people found they could no longer remain there. So they left, by whatever means they could find. They didn't care where they were going: their only thought was to get away.

Many put to sea in unseaworthy small boats, without sufficient food or water, drifting day after day. Winds and currents took them southwards, where many of the overcrowded vessels foundered in fierce tropical storms or were prey to pirates. Some managed to stay afloat until they drifted ashore in southern Thailand, Indonesia, Malaysia and even the northern coast of Australia.

The Boat People, as the refugees came to be called, were placed in holding camps throughout South-East Asia while attempts were made to find them permanent homes. Many eventually made their way to Australia, where today there is a large, and growing, Vietnamese community, grappling with all the problems of life in a culture that is different from their own. Some have never completely made the transition. Their hearts are still in Vietnam, or in a leaking, sinking boat, with the loved ones whom they have left behind.

ONE

The seaplane swept in low from the sea, lifted a little over the coconut palms that lined the beach, and then angled sharply into a steep turn above the resort buildings. The clatter of its engine shattered the early morning calm, disturbing a flock of cockatoos which rose from the trees and flapped about untidily like bits of white paper blowing in its slipstream, screeching defiance and alarm.

'Mary! Mail plane's in!' Greg swept into the family-room of the Wilsons' private quarters, almost knocking Mary Travers off her feet.

'Tell Sally, not me.' Mary was not impressed. She was looking with some trepidation towards the pine dresser, where several cups, dislodged by the vibrations of the plane's passage, had moved dangerously close to the edge of the top shelf. She called after him, urgently, 'And don't slam the . . . !'

But she was too late. Greg had gone, and for the crockery the impact as the door closed explosively behind him was the final straw. A cup teetered on the brink, then fell, but with lightning reflexes and a sense of anticipation unequalled by any Test cricketer, the housekeeper lunged and was there before it reached the floor. She caught it cleanly, replaced it, and then, one by one, moved its companions back to their original positions. Slightly out of breath, but otherwise unperturbed, she stood back and looked at them, all in a row, out of harm's way once again.

Then she went on setting the table for breakfast: Mary was quite accustomed to low-flying planes and impatient fourteen-year-old boys.

Outside, Greg looked for the plane, but it was long gone, so he set off for the beach. The sandy pathway which lead from the manager's private quarters meandered among hibiscus bushes and sweet-smelling frangipanni trees, linking the holiday lodges with the main buildings of the resort, and several sleepy-eyed guests, no doubt rudely awakened by the plane, were standing at their doors in various states of undress. Greg looked at his watch: a quarter to eight: time they were up and about, anyway. He smiled and said 'Hi' as he passed.

It was like that on Butterfly Island; you were friends with everyone, even if you'd only met them minutes before. It was part and parcel of living on an island resort. Outside the main building he heard the rattle of crockery and smelt the friendly aroma of hot coffee and freshly-made toast coming from the dining-room; splashes and laughter in the nearby pool told him that some guests were enjoying a pre-breakfast swim. There was a loud squeal, and Greg grinned: maybe it wasn't a pre-breakfast swim; may be they were still partying-on from the night before!

He moved on towards the beach. It was very still, warm, and humid, even at this early hour, and the sea was glassy-smooth; sure signs of another hot, sticky day. His sister Sally was standing at the edge of a clump of palms, looking out across the lagoon towards the west, where the distant mountains floated serenely above the early morning mist.

Sally was seventeen, a brunette, with an open, friendly face, and big brown eyes. Like Greg, she had an ever-ready smile and a deep, long-term suntan that no pallid southern tourist could ever hope to acquire, even after a month's holiday on the Great Barrier Reef. Her attention was focused on a small, light-coloured dot sliding across the darker background of the smoke from last night's canefield fires on the mainland, fifteen kilometres away, and Greg picked it up at once. It was the plane, coming back.

He stood beside her as the dot came closer, straining his eyes until he could distinguish the wings and the tail, and then suddenly he was conscious once again of the noise, rising from a distant drone to a rapidly increasing, full-throated, pulsating roar.

He grinned at her, a positive identification made: that engine mounted above the wing was a dead give-away. 'The Buccaneer,' he exclaimed, raising his voice above the racket.

'It's Bob!' Sally replied, and ran down the sand so that she could be seen, waving excitedly as the amphibian came on low across the lagoon. The pilot waggled the wings in reply, and they caught just a glimpse of his tanned, smiling face as he put the plane into another steep turn almost overhead.

Suddenly the clatter of the engine died away, and the machine began to lose height rapidly, until the hull kissed the calm surface of the bay, parting the water cleanly and settling as the machine lost flying speed. It turned and headed back towards them, and as it surged across the shallows Greg saw the wheels unfold from the lower surface of the wing before the seaplane heaved itself out of the water and waddled up the sand like an ungainly duck. The propeller clicked to a stop. Suddenly it was very quiet, the only sounds being the distant protests of the still-indignant cocka-toos.

The hatch opened and Bob Gallio dropped lightly on to the sand. 'Long time no see,' he grinned, coming up the beach towards them. He was a few years older than Sally, darkly handsome, and wearing the standard uniform of an island charter pilot: dark shorts and a white shirt, with the flying fish emblem of Gallio-Air emblazoned on the pocket.

Sally smiled back. 'Sure . . . all of forty-three hours.'

His grin broadened. 'That's too long.'

Greg interrupted. 'Hiya, Bob. Can I get the parcels?' All this smooth talk made him sick.

The pilot waved him towards the plane. 'Go for your life.' As Greg moved over to open the nose locker, Bob and Sally walked together up the beach, hand in hand.

'What kind of mood is your dad in?' Bob asked.

Sally threw him a sidelong glance. 'Why?'

'Because I've got something for him.' Bob reached behind the multi-coloured flying fish and produced an envelope. 'Special delivery,' he said, holding it up, and Sally knew what it was at once: a Gallio-Air account.

'Special delivery?' she said, puzzled.

'You were supposed to pay it a month ago, Sal,' Bob said quietly.

Suddenly she stopped walking. 'Honestly, your father's the limit!' she said.

Bob was taken aback. He had expected defence, not attack. 'Hang on! He's got bills to pay too, you know.'

She let go his hand and turned to face him, eyes blazing. 'My dad's a bad risk, is that it?'

'Come on, Sal. Stop treating me like a debt collector.'

'Well, aren't you?'

He decided to change tack; getting mad was getting them nowhere. 'Come on, Sal. My old man thinks the world of your dad, you know that. It's business, that's all.'

He was right and Sally knew it. Her father and Sergio Gallio had been friends, as well as business associates, for a long time. There was silence while she stood quietly, thoughtfully, feeling a bit lost, looking down at the sand. Finally she spoke: 'It wouldn't be so bad, if your bill was the only one.' He took her hand sympathetically and they walked together up the sand.

They found Charlie Wilson in the workshop, a ramshackle old shed under some she-oak trees, not far from the main building. It was the oldest structure on the island; Sally's grandfather, Old Man Wilson, had built it, and lived in it, when he first came to Butterfly. That was over fifty years ago, and it was showing its age.

Inside, it was a mess. There was stuff everywhere; paint tins and timber and tools, bits of outboard motors, fishing nets, fishing tackle, oars, sails and spars, bottles of nuts and bolts and boxes of rusty nails, rolls of chicken wire and bags of cement. A pair of casement windows leant against one wall; they'd been there for as long as Sally could remember, forever awaiting repair. But despite the apparent disarray, Charlie always seemed to know where everything was. Amidst the chaos, there was a place for everything, and as far as he was concerned, everything was in its place. Sally and Mary had tried to tidy up, just once, to their cost. The workshop was Charlie's domain, and woe betide anyone who attempted to interfere!

He didn't see them when they came in, because he was wearing a face mask, welding, repairing a metal gate. In the intense, eerie blue-white glare flickering around the old shed he could have been Ned Kelly, the bushranger, come back to haunt them, but the illusion was spoiled by the sweat-stained singlet and faded jeans.

They looked away, trying to ignore the hypnotic attraction of the searing flame, listening instead to the spit and crackle of the sparks cascading on to the concrete floor. Then, suddenly, the glare was gone, and the shed seemed very dark. As they turned back towards him Charlie lifted the shield and became aware of their presence for the first time.

His craggy features broke into a welcoming smile. 'G'day, Bob! I thought I heard you buzzing around!'

He took the envelope and ripped it open. Bob watched

as he read it. Charlie wasn't a big man, but he was wiry, and fit, and hardened by years of healthy outdoor work. Rivulets of sweat trickled down his forehead as he rapidly scanned the account. The smile disappeared.

'Sorry about this, Mr Wilson,' said Bob, embarrassed.

Charlie dismissed his apology with a wave. 'Your dad's company provides a service, and I expect to pay for it.' He smiled again, grimly now. 'Mind you, I didn't expect to pay for it so soon, but there you go.'

He tossed the paper on to the bench, and Sally could make out one word, in big, red, untidy letters: 'OVERDUE' scrawled over the face of the neatly type-written account. She recognised Sergio Gallio's hand-writing, and it made her angry.

There was an awkward silence that Bob felt compelled to fill. 'Dad's got his commitments,' he said lamely. As the words were coming out, he knew he'd made a mistake, said too much, but it was too late. Charlie looked at him sharply. Bob waited for the axe to fall.

But it didn't. Instead, Charlie suddenly grinned, taking pity on him. 'Stop looking like a condemned man!' he said. 'What did you think I was going to say?'

Bob shrugged.

Charlie went on. 'It's not the end of the world, you know.'

'No . . .' Bob began.

'Come on,' Charlie continued, cutting him short. 'Let's go and have some breakfast.' And with that he was gone.

Much relieved, Bob winked at Sally as they followed him outside.

Jackie Wilson, the youngest member of the Wilson family, stood under the paw paw trees, feeding her birds. She had heard the Buccaneer come over, but she hadn't bothered to go down to meet it, because she was

12

busy. First things first, the birds were a big responsibility. They weren't really *her* birds, since they were
completely free to come and go as they pleased; rainbow
lorikeets, the brilliantly-coloured scarlet and green
parrots that lived in the bush which clothed most of
Butterfly Island. Rainbow lorikeets had a sweet tooth
(just an expression . . . everyone knew birds didn't have
actual teeth), and they couldn't resist the bread and
honey that Jackie offered them from a tin plate, twice a
day. She'd become quite a tourist attraction herself
among the resort guests as she stood, plate in hand,
festooned with lorikeets; on her shoulders, her arms, her
head, nibbling at the honey (and sometimes her ears)
completely unafraid. Not bad for a twelve-year-old.

She'd started the ritual by herself, about two years
ago. It was a bit of a nuisance sometimes, doing it every
day, especially when it rained, but as Charlie had
pointed out, once you start something like this and the
birds become dependent upon you for food, that's it.
You're committed. You can't let them down.

'Jack-ee!'

Alarmed, the birds took flight in a blur of red and
green and circled in confusion. Jackie bit her lip,
annoyed. She always knew that Greg was coming long
before he appeared.

He entered the clearing at a brisk trot and came over
to her, completely ignoring the screeching parrots now
protesting noisily from the nearby trees. 'Dad says
come and have your breakfast!' he announced self-
importantly, but Jackie made no move to comply.
Instead, she held up the plate, trying to entice the
lorikeets back down. 'Come on!' insisted Greg. 'We'll be
late.'

'All right! All right!' she snapped, then pouted. 'You
wouldn't be in such a hurry if it was *your* tooth.' She had
a dental appointment this morning, in Ellis River. It
was only a small filling, but it would mean a needle, just

13

the same, and the mere thought of it gave her the creeps.

Greg was unsympathetic; in fact he was off again already, but a short distance down the path he stopped and looked back. 'Jackie! Come *on!*'

She scowled. All *he* wanted was to get his hands on *Elizabeth*.

Named after their mother, the *Elizabeth* was Butterfly's motor launch; fifteen metres long, powered by twin diesels, and fitted with radio, radar, an echo-sounder, and a lot of other expensive navigational gear. An elegant vessel, she was Charlie Wilson's pride and joy. Normally he wouldn't allow anyone else near her, but he was very busy today, because apart from normal routine chores, he had to help Sally finish off the new brochure for the resort. It was one of those unavoidable rush jobs, so today Greg was taking *Elizabeth* across to town, on his own for the very first time. It was a big responsibility, but he'd been around boats all his life, and he knew he was equal to the task. It was obvious that his father thought so, too, and that meant a lot.

An hour later, Bob and Sally saw them off at the jetty. Greg stood at the wheel, shouting orders at Jackie as she moved about on deck, casting off. She pouted. She knew her way around *Elizabeth*, too, and knew what to do without anybody yelling at her, but this was Greg's big day, and he was making the most of it.

'Let go forra'd!' Greg yelled, but she'd already done it, and was coiling the rope neatly on the deck, muttering to herself through clenched teeth.

'Young Greg had better watch it, or he'll have a mutiny on his hands,' grinned Bob as *Elizabeth* slid slowly away from the jetty then began to turn, heading out into the bay. With a final wave he took Sally's hand and they strolled back together along the jetty towards the beach.

When they reached the pathway that led through the cool shadows of the coconut palms back towards the main building, Sally stopped and turned to face him. 'I've got to get back,' she said, softly, 'Dad'll have kittens if I don't make a start on that brochure soon.'

Bob nodded. 'He's had enough agro for one day,' he said ruefully.

Sally knew that he was still thinking of the overdue account, and she appreciated his concern. She reached up and kissed him. 'Forget it,' she said softly. 'You were only doing your job.'

But it wasn't as easy as that. Bob found himself running over the morning's events a short time later as he sat in the Buccaneer, listening to the engine grumbling away behind him, and feeling the machine lift easily over the slight swell. He was heading towards his take-off point, out in the bay, and he was far from pleased with himself.

Sally had been right; he was little more than a debt collector, doing his dad's dirty work, and he'd made a mess of it into the bargain. The Wilsons were having a hard time: he'd known that. He should have just handed over the envelope and kept his big mouth shut! Charlie was a good bloke, to let it go like that. He grinned ruefully at the recollection. Sally had given him some stick, but he was off the hook now. He remembered the goodbye kiss and grinned again.

He was well offshore now, and he turned back towards Butterfly Island, into the wind, and carried out his checks, his hands running over the controls with practised ease. Bob was a good pilot, and he knew it, but he was also well aware that over-confidence was a potentially fatal state of mind for anyone who flew. The sky, like the sea, was totally unforgiving. Checks completed, he picked up the microphone and notified the controller in Cairns, two hundred kilometres away, of his intentions. The response came at once, loud and clear, and he pushed the throttle forward smoothly, all the way.

The engine's grumble became a full-throated howl and the Buccaneer shuddered and buried her head, covering the windscreen in a shower of spray. The water was reluctant to let her go, but Bob had other ideas. He worked the controls, coaxing her, helping her, bullying her, until the perspex began to clear as she lifted ahead of her bow wave and began to plane like a speedboat over the surface of the sea which was now beating a furious but futile tattoo on the thin aluminium hull. Then, suddenly the drumming stopped and he knew they'd made the transition. She was free. She wanted to climb but he held her down, just above the surface, gaining speed, while the island came closer and closer, and then, when the time was right, he eased her up, and the beach and coconut palms swept by below. He put her into a gentle, climbing turn, and watched the wing tip describe a lazy arc around the resort buildings, nestling among the trees. Outside the main building he saw a tiny figure, waving. Sally. He rocked the wings from side to side in reply, and then she and Butterfly Island were gone, and he was bearing down upon *Elizabeth*, now well offshore, her wake gunbarrel-straight behind her. Bob grinned: young Greg would be taking great pride in that. He rocked the wings again as the launch swept by below and was lost to view behind the wing. He looked ahead. The mainland lay ten minutes away, to the west, but meantime there were islands all around him; emerald green hummocks in a brilliant sapphire sea, with here and there a crescent of bright yellow sand bordering a secluded bay. He knew that the islands were really the tops of ancient mountains, submerged when the sea level rose thousands of years ago; he also knew that in the warm, shallow tropic sea all around them, millions upon millions of tiny polyps had laboured through countless generations to construct coral reefs. These fringing reefs were easily visible from this height as shades of purple and pale

16

green beneath the ocean's brilliant blue, broken briefly here and there by the white gleam of a breaking wave. Bob breathed a deep, contented sigh, and let it all soak in. He'd flown this route many times, carrying hundreds of tourists to and from the Great Barrier Reef, but a view like that could never become routine.

He crossed the coast above the mouth of the Ellis River and began to descend, following its snaking curves inland, over mudflats and mangrove swamps towards the town that shared its name. He was over lush green sugar canefields now, stretching away across the narrow coastal plane to the jungle-clad ramparts of the Great Dividing Range. Bob made a neat, steep turn around the chimney of the Ellis River Sugar Mill, coming down rapidly now, the plane lurching and dropping sickeningly in the mid-morning turbulence over the town's wide streets and galvanised iron roofs. He lined up for landing, wheels and flaps down, and thirty seconds later he was on the ground, breathing in the hot, humid, sweet-smelling air.

By modern standards, Ellis River Airport hardly qualified for the name. The single runway, thrusting out into the desolation of a reclaimed mangrove swamp, had been built originally during the Second World War. It had been lengthened in recent years to accommodate the big jets, bringing in tourists from down south, but apart from that little had changed in forty years; certainly not the buildings, a motley collection of igloo-style hangars and sheds.

Bob taxied the Buccaneer among a gaggle of assorted light aircraft and brought it to a nodding halt outside a long, low, wooden building that sported a coat of bright paint and a few superficial alterations in an attempt to conceal its military origins. There was a large sign on the roof: GALLIO AIR. AIR CHARTER. TOURIST FLIGHTS TO THE GREAT BARRIER REEF.'

As the engine spluttered to a halt his father came out

of his office and hurried across the tarmac. Sergio Gallio was a short, thick-set man, with a receding hairline and double chins. 'Did you give it to him?' he asked anxiously.

Bob grinned to himself as he unbuckled his seat belt. His father was a born worrier. He worried about everything; about the cost of aviation fuel, about sugar prices, about the weather, about the competition, about maintenance, about spares, advertising, tractor prices, and a hundred and one other things. On the rare occasions when things were going well he worried about not worrying, too. And now, Bob knew, he was worrying about a friend.

'Roberto, I ask you a question!' his father repeated, waving his arms in the air.

'Yes, I gave it to him,' replied Bob.

'And what did he say?'

'He said he'll pay.'

'And that is all?'

Bob nodded. 'Yep.'

'Surely he said some other things?' pressed Sergio, but Bob had had enough.

'Look, Dad, gi'mme a break,' he said wearily. It had been a tough morning. 'From now on, you handle the bills and I fly the planes. OK?'

Before Sergio had a chance to reply a sudden movement broke his train of thought, and he saw a small figure scurry across the tarmac and disappear behind a pile of fuel drums stacked along the hangar wall. He scowled. Trespassers hanging around his aeroplanes he didn't need; especially kids. 'Hey, you! What you doing?' he yelled, and hurried forward, but before he could reach the drums the figure broke cover again. It was a boy. He paused for a moment and then was gone, running like a frightened jackrabbit towards the main road. Sergio shook a fist after him. 'And don'ta you come back, eh!'

Father and son stood side by side, watching, until the fugitive had disappeared.

It seemed to Vo Diem that he'd been running all his life, but he kept going, his feet pounding on the bitumen, driven by anger as well as fear. He was angry with himself; he'd been damn stupid letting that old guy see him; he'd blown his chances of getting out by air. Now he'd have to get back to the town and try to find another way.

A short distance away there was a cattle grid, and then a T-junction, where the airport access road joined the main highway. Diem paused, gasping for breath, and watched the traffic speeding to and fro. Too busy to be safe out there. He looked around for another, more secure route.

He soon found one. Sugar cane grew right to the edge of the road; a man-made jungle two metres high. Perfect cover! He slipped through the barbed wire fence and pushed his way into the thick, purple-brown stalks until they closed behind him, and then turned and moved along parallel to the road, shielded from view. It was safe, but slow, forcing a way through the cane, and after a short while he suddenly felt very tired. He sank on to the soft ground and lay back, looking up through the cool green leaves at graceful sugar cane tassels waving against the pale blue sky. How long had he been on the run? He tried to count up: a day and two nights on the freight train, or was it one night and two days? It seemed like a hundred years. He remembered climbing out of the wagon: was it yesterday or today? Yes. Today. This morning. He had stood there, in the dust of the railway yard, relishing the taste and smell of the tropical air for the first time in many months. He remembered how good that had made him feel, and he breathed in deeply again. It was still there; that warm, moist, soft, sweet, spicy, exciting tang, and it made him feel at home. He closed his eyes, content, ignoring the hunger pains that were gnawing away at his insides, and fell asleep.

Jackie stood at *Elizabeth's* bow, comfortably braced against the gentle rise and fall of the deck, breathing the salty air, and enjoying the occasional dollops of spray that slapped on to her face and neck and bare brown legs. The mainland lay only a kilometre or so ahead now, but she seldom looked in that direction, preferring instead to lean out over the rail so that she could see the wake, a temporary, drifting record of their passage, stretching all the way back to Butterfly Island, which was now a smudge in the blue distance, far astern. She leaned further over the side and looked down. From time to time, just in front of the creaming bow wave, a tiny fish would spear out of the water and glide on miniature wings, inches above the surface, for fifty metres or more like a silver insect, before disappearing once again with scarcely a splash; flying fish, alarmed by the launch bearing down on them, employing the only defence mechanism they knew.

As *Elizabeth* entered the mouth of the Ellis River, Jackie went aft to join Greg, who stood in the wheelhouse, relaxed yet alert, feeding the smooth, highly-polished wood and brass ship's wheel from hand to hand. Jackie grinned to herself: he was having a great time!

As they motored slowly upstream the water lost its blue colour and became a muddy brown. There were mangrove swamps on either bank; low, green and mysterious, the mangrove trees levering themselves out of the mud in a grotesque tangle of twisted, exposed roots and sharp spikes, sprouting, fanglike, from the ooze. Jackie shuddered: crocodile country.

They rounded a bend, and there were the roofs and buildings of Ellis River, reaching down to the water's edge. There were advertising signs too, exhorting them to *Drink Coca Cola*, and *Eat Kentucky Fried* and *Bank Commonwealth* and *Keep Australia Beautiful* and *See the Barrier Reef With Gallio-Air*. Civilisation. Greg throttled right back, taking it easy. He wasn't going to foul things up now. He anxiously studied the marina ahead, then breathed a sigh of relief: most of the tourist boats were out, and there were several adjacent, empty berths, leaving him plenty of room to manoeuvre. He spun the wheel and *Elizabeth* responded, turning in a wide arc until her bow was facing once again out to sea. He manipulated the throttles, running the engines astern to check the speed, and then inching ahead again, easing her in. With the fast-running tide it was a difficult manoeuvre, but he accomplished it with great skill, and *Elizabeth* edged up to the wharf with the gentlest of bumps. He was concentrating so hard that he forgot to order Jackie to make fast, but she did it anyway, deftly tossing a rope over a mooring pile forrard and securing it with a flick of the wrist, then running aft to do the same thing at the stern.

Greg switched off and stood at the open wheelhouse door, watching as she came back. 'I'll meet you back here when the dentist has finished with you,' he said, rubbing his hands in mock glee. He whistled shrilly, imitating the sound of the drill.

Jackie was not amused. 'Thanks heaps, Greg.'

As she stepped nimbly ashore, Greg called after her, rubbing it in: 'Open wide!'

She grabbed a handful of seaweed lying on the wharf. It was wet, rotten, and very smelly; just the thing. She caught a nauseating whiff herself as she drew back her arm and let fly. It was an accurate throw, but her brother ducked and came up, grinning, still making that infuriating whistling sound. Jackie scowled at him and stormed off. Chuckling to himself, Greg checked the mooring ropes, filling in time until she was out of sight, then he too stepped ashore and made off towards the town.

Vo Diem couldn't breathe; his throat was burning and dry, and an acrid smell seemed to be eating away the insides of his nose. Gasping for air, he began to cough, and the effort jerked him half-awake. He sat bolt upright, disorientated, eyes wide open with fear. They immediately began to stream with tears, but not before he recognised the source of his discomfort. *Smoke.* Thick, acrid, suffocating smoke; and beyond that, not far away, he could hear the unmistakable crackle and roar of flames. He jumped to his feet, close to panic. He knew about fire. Once again he saw the Phantom bomber bearing down, full of silent menace, as if in a dream; once again he watched the four black drums detach themselves and fall, tumbling in a graceful arc until they met the earth, instantly erupting in a huge orange fireball, ballooning towards him with awesome speed. Once again he felt the heat, searing his legs, his arms, his cheeks, and his forehead, and it was too much to bear.

Vo Diem turned and ran.

Yet the nightmare images came after him; the huts of his village, enveloped in all-consuming flames; children he knew, friends he played with, screaming in terror and pain. He saw his mother and father. . . .

Suddenly he was clear – the smoke was gone, the fire left behind. He continued to run, past the point of exhaustion, his legs driven only by his fear. At last he had to stop, heart pounding, hands on knees, greedily gulping fresh air. When eventually, partially recovered, he made himself look back, it was not to a flaming village in South Vietnam, but a sugar canefield burning in North Queensland, Australia. It was a peaceful blaze, started not by napalm, but by a group of work-men, whom he could see in the distance, torches in hand, firing the sugar cane to clear away the under-growth before it was cut. He'd noticed similar fields, and fires, before, from the train. It was obvious that the men hadn't spotted him yet, so he quickly crossed the road and disappeared into the opposite field.

It took him about twenty minutes to reach the town, and his cover disappeared with the canefields, because, like most Queensland country towns, Ellis River had wide streets, each with a broad expanse of bare dirt on either side of a central strip of bitumen and few places to hide. And then it rained, a short, sharp, tropical down-pour, forcing him to seek shelter under one of the houses. Most of the single-storey houses were set up high, on concrete posts, to take advantage of every breath of cooling breeze, and to provide space for storing junk and drying clothes in the wet season. It reminded Diem of houses in his village, back home in Vietnam. They were built up on stilts, too; or they had been, before the helicopters came. . . . A dog sniffed him out and began to bark, so he left, running out into the street to be instantly soaked to the skin, but it was warm rain, and anyway the sun suddenly came out and in ten minutes he was dry again. Dry, and hungry.

He stopped underneath the deep shade of a mango tree. It was early in the season, but already the ground was littered with fallen mangoes and the humid midday air reeked with the stench of over-ripe and rotting fruit. The street was deserted, so Diem took his time and ate his fill, savouring the sweet, delicate flavour and enjoy-ing the decadent sensation of the aromatic juice dribbling down his chin. Satisfied, he set off again, heading towards the taller buldings which identified the business centre of the town. The main street was bordered with stately palms and was wide enough to accommodate a central garden of hibiscus and hot pink bougainvillea; more colour was provided by striped canvas shop-front awnings that flapped in the warm breeze. The street was lined with parked cars and trucks. He felt secure here because there were people about and he knew that, if necessary, he could vanish in a second, swallowed up in the crowd. A police car cruised across an intersection ahead and he almost panicked and put his theory to the test, but managed to keep his self-control, and the car kept going. As he turned a corner, a familiar shape caught his eye: a Coke bottle, twenty feet high, on an advertising hoarding. Vo Diem grinned to himself; it was exactly the same advertisement that he'd seen many times in Vietnam. And then, behind the sign, through the trees, he saw the gleam of water.

Water! Boats! Things were looking up. He ran down the slight hill leading to the waterfront and scanned the marina with a practised eye. There were one or two yachts tied up, but he dismissed these at once as impracticable; they would have to be sailed; and in any case they were too slow. There were several trawlers, but they would probably have crew members aboard. His eye was drawn to another vessel, about fifteen metres long, obviously seaworthy, and apparently deserted: definitely worth a closer look.

Diem broke cover, walked quickly down the gangway, along the jetty, and with a quick backward glance to see if he'd been spotted, stepped casually aboard. He went straight to the wheelhouse. He knew what he was looking for, and his heart leapt with excitement when he saw that they were there; keys; hanging in the ignition lock. He hurried to the bow of the boat and cast off the mooring ropes, then ran aft and let go at the stern, feeling the vessel begin to drift at once with the tide. Back in the wheelhouse he took a deep breath, turned the key, then pressed one of the two starter buttons, hard. Somewhere beneath his feet he heard a rumble as the big diesel began to turn. He pressed the second button.

'Hey!' A girl was standing in the hatchway. 'What do you think *you're* doing?'

Vo Diem was in no mood to answer questions, and with a vicious shove he sent Jackie tumbling backwards down the companionway, to land painfully on the deck. He slammed the hatchcover closed, muffling the cries that quickly began to emanate from below.

'Let me out! Help! Help!' She began hammering on the door, but he ignored her protests, and slammed the gear levers forward, at the same time expertly spinning the wheel. The diesels responded with a roar, and *Elizabeth* moved out into the channel, heading for the open sea.

TWO

Whistling happily but grossly out of tune, Greg Wilson lugged a sugar bag full of supplies along the footpath. Greg always enjoyed coming across to Ellis River. It was only a small town; he knew that, but to him it was a metropolis, full of life, and amidst its casual hustle and bustle he felt that he belonged to the outside world.

Today had been extra special; a great day: and to celebrate his first crossing in total command of *Elizabeth* he'd gone around to the *New Paris* Café and Milk Bar, and looked up a few mates. He usually did this anyway when he came across to town, because one thing Greg lacked was the company of guys his own age. There were always plenty of teenage kids at the resort, but you never got to know them; they were here one day and gone the next; and he didn't meet anyone at school, because he didn't go; Greg did his lessons by correspondence, not the best way to eyeball people. Now he was late, because Nick, the owner of the *New Paris*, had recently installed a couple of electronic pinball machines, and the time had just sort of run away. Tough! It wouldn't hurt Jackie to wait.

Suddenly it became patently obvious that she hadn't.

He stopped dead in his tracks, the tune evaporating from his lips. The berth where he'd left *Elizabeth* was empty! Dropping the supplies in a heap on the pavement, he broke into a run, and with a sinking feeling in his stomach, sprinted down the jetty to the gaping space. He looked up and down the river, but of the launch there was no sign. Greg's brow furrowed. That Jackie! He'd given her a hard time about the dentist, but pinching the boat to get back at him was going too far!

Suddenly he realised that Jackie couldn't have taken *Elizabeth*, because *he* had the keys.

Or *did* he?

His heart missed a beat and he began to search frantically, panic mounting, the empty feeling in his stomach intensifying as his fingers fumbled vainly through each pocket in turn. Already Greg could hear Charlie's angry voice; 'What a stupid, careless, irresponsible thing to do!' and automatically his mind began to race. It wasn't his fault; it was Jackie's. She had no right to take the boat, just because he was a few minutes late. . . .

He despised himself immediately. What a gutless wonder he was! Charlie had left him in charge. He'd been responsible, and he'd blown it. It was as simple as that. Now, instead of wasting time thinking up pathetic excuses, he had to get after Jackie as quickly as he could. And when he caught her, *if* he caught her. . . .

He looked around. Johnson's boatyard was about a hundred yards away, and he raced for that, hurdling the upturned hulls and dodging around the cradled yachts and cruisers undergoing storage or repair. Greg spotted his target inside the big galvanised shed; a short, stocky man in overalls, working on an outboard motor.

'Lofty!' The little man's nickname was a standing joke around Ellis River, but Greg wasn't laughing now. 'Lofty! Jackie's gone!' The boy jerked the words out, explaining the position as quickly as he could, between gulps of air.

'Take it easy, son.' The mechanic tried to settle him down, but Greg was in no mood for reassurance.

'Take it *easy*! She's only twelve! Dad's gonna *kill* me!'

Five minutes later he was standing on the flybridge of Johnson's big Bertram, racing downriver, Lofty at the wheel, expecting to overtake the *Elizabeth* at every turn, but at each bend the mangroves slid aside to reveal nothing but yet another stretch of vacant water. Soon the horizon began to widen as they entered the broader expanse of the open sea, and Greg peered anxiously ahead as the cruiser lifted easily over the first swell and crashed into the trough on the other side in a cloud of spray.

Nothing.

On the radar there was one big blip, easily identified as a tourist boat heading home, but of *Elizabeth* there was no sign. She was probably on the far side of one of the islands, away from the probing electronic beam. They couldn't possibly search behind them all. Serious-faced, Lofty Johnson flicked the switch on the two-way radio, caught Greg's eye, and pointed to the mike. It wasn't a suggestion; it was a command, and the boy gritted his teeth as he uncradled it. Lofty was right; it was time Charlie was told.

Jackie had been hammering on the cabin door for hours, or so it seemed; not that it had done her any good. The boy had taken no notice of her whatsoever, not an easy thing to do, because she'd given the door quite a pounding, but she was exhausted now, sitting huddled on the bottom step. Scared, too; and for the first time she allowed herself a little cry: but only for a moment, because almost as soon as she started she realised what little good *that* would do. She climbed back up the three steps, but this time, instead of banging with her fists, she put an eye to a chink in the door. Her heart jumped. He was staring straight back at her!

Jackie swallowed hard and put on an accusing voice:

'You're in big trouble, you know. This is stealing!' The boy just stared back, impassively. No reaction at all; no indication that he'd understood a single word. Jackie studied him as he stood at the wheel, totally ignoring her presence on the other side of the door.

He was about Greg's age; fourteen; maybe a bit older; dark-haired, with slanting, oriental eyes below thick, bushy brows. At first she thought he was Chinese, but there was something about him that told her that he wasn't. Japanese? Korean? Jackie shrugged. Who cared where he came *from*? What mattered was where he was going *to*, because like it or not, she was being taken along for the ride.

She decided on another approach, and pressed her lips up against the crack in the door, putting on her most appealing voice, the one that worked so often with Greg and her dad.

'Listen . . . if you take me straight back to Ellis River, I won't tell on you. I promise . . . cross my heart.'

He didn't even blink a response.

Suddenly the two-way speaker mounted on the cabin roof crackled into life: 'VK4 ELB, VK4 ELB . . . Butterfly Island launch. . . . Do you read me, Jackie? Over.'

Her spirits soared. 'That's my dad!' Jackie yelled the words through the door, but the boy continued to ignore her, so she had to sit, fists clenched with frustration, listening helplessly as Charlie tried again.

'VK4 ELB, VK4 ELB . . . Butterfly Island launch. . . . Do you read me, Jackie? Over.'

The sound of his voice, so near and yet so far, was almost too much for Jackie to bear, and she launched another concerted attack against the door, hammering and yelling at the same time: 'That's my father! My father! Don't you understand? He knows where we are, and he'll be after you. You've gotta take me back!' Her outburst had some effect this time, and his eyes flickered

29

under the onslaught of blows and yelled words, giving Jackie some satisfaction, so she doubled her efforts, but there was no further response. Gradually her threats and pleas died away, and then the hammering ceased, too. Jackie sat once again on the steps, head on knees, utterly exhausted, very scared, not knowing what else she could do.

Exactly how long she sat there she wasn't sure, because she felt all feverish and unreal; but when the engine note suddenly slowed the abrupt change in sound brought back her energy at once, and she jumped to her feet, ran to a porthole, and looked out.

Coral; light-brown, brick-red, purple-green, stretched as far as the eye could see. Jackie quickly crossed the cabin and looked through a porthole on the opposite side: coral there, too. At once she knew where they were; the Outer Barrier; a vast expanse of reef, exposed at low tide, criss-crossed by a maze of channels, most of them dead ends. It took specialised knowledge, and a lot of experience, to get through here to the open sea; experience that this kid wouldn't have; she'd bet on it.

She ran up the steps and called through the door, 'You'll never make it, you know.'

There was no reply. How unusual!

She tried again, speaking very slowly, as if to a young child: 'This is the Barrier Reef . . . Barrier . . . you know? There is no way through.' She found herself making hand gestures to reinforce the words, even though she knew he couldn't see them through the door. The boy responded by reaching for the throttles and slowing the engines further. The *Elizabeth* was barely moving now, and through the portholes Jackie watched as the coral moved closer and closer on either side, until she felt she could reach out and touch it.

Bump! *Crunch*!

She'd been expecting the impact, but when it happened it was a shock just the same; *Elizabeth* came to a grinding halt, and Jackie heard the engines rev up, then slow, then stop. Footsteps ran along the deck above her head, heading towards the bow; then there was silence, except for the 'lap, slap' of wavelets against the hull. She moved over to the porthole and angled her head against the glass, peering as far ahead of the *Elizabeth* as she could. About a hundred yards away she caught sight of the boy, scrambling across the reef; falling into shallow pools, clambering to his feet only to get up and fall again. Jackie bit her lip; if he kept that up the razor-sharp coral would cut him to pieces; and coral cuts became infected very easily; she knew that from painful experience!

As she watched, the boy seemed to reach the same conclusion, because he stopped, looked down at his legs, then back at the launch, then seawards, towards the outer edge of the reef, where the Pacific rollers were dashing themselves against the coral ramparts, releasing in a split second all the energy they had built up as they travelled, unimpeded, across thousands of kilometres of open sea. And then, suddenly, she couldn't see him any more because he had stumbled on, passing from her field of view.

Jackie didn't waste time; there wasn't much future for him out there, stumbling about on the reef; he'd be back, sooner rather than later, so there wasn't a second to lose. Grabbing a teaspoon from the galley locker, she slipped it through the crack between the jamb and the door and pushed hard against the catch on the outside. It opened easily and in an instant she was through, making for the radio.

'VK4 BIR, VK4 BIR . . . Butterfly Island . . . do you read me? It's Jackie, Dad. Over.'

The reply came back at once. 'Reading you, Jackie. What the devil do you think you're up to? Over.'

She glanced quickly around the horizon, trying to find a landmark, until a familiar shape came into view about a kilometre astern; a smudge of low scrub atop a white crescent of sand, completely surrounded by a pale, copper-green lagoon, in turn bounded by exposed coral. Things were looking up! She smiled to herself as she pressed the transmit button once more. 'I'm a bit south of Spencer's Cay . . . over.'

The speaker almost vibrated itself off its mountings as Charlie's enraged reply came through: 'Spencer's Cay! That's halfway to Fiji! You've got a lot of questions to answer, young lady! We're on our way. Over and out!'

Jackie replaced the microphone on its cradle, and moved outside to the rail. *Elizabeth* was OK. She wasn't very high on the reef, and she'd float off easily in a couple of hours with the tide coming in. The sea was surging over the coral with each incoming wave, flooding the shallow pools, then dropping away, sucked back into the ocean depths, leaving dozens of rushing cascades.

Jackie glanced up at the sky. In a few hours it would be dark, and this would be a dangerous place, completely covered by the sea. She shivered, and not from cold. She hoped she wasn't here then; the reef was beautiful, and fascinating, and all the other words the tourist brochures used, but sometimes it could be very lonely and creepy, too.

The radio was silent now, but that didn't matter. It had served its purpose, and Jackie knew that her father was on his way. He'd get out here, and rescue her, somehow. All she had to do, all she *could* do, was wait.

She looked across at the reef once more. The boy was sitting motionless on a bommie, a coral outcrop higher than the rest, with the rising tide surging around his feet. Jackie felt sorry for him. He looked like a shag on a rock, with one important difference: when the water threatened to swallow its perch a *real* shag could simply spread its wings and fly away. She shivered again: her dad had better get here soon!

An hour passed. The tide was higher now, and Jackie could feel *Elizabeth* becoming more buoyant, lifting on each incoming swell, trying hard to float, then dropping back on to the reef with a resounding crunch and a shock that shook her from stem to stern. Jackie bit her lip. As long as the coral broke and not the boat, things would be OK; but it couldn't go on for long; many a vessel had pounded itself to pieces on the reef.

Another swell came. The *Elizabeth* lifted, then dropped, and Jackie braced herself against yet another crash, but this time, as the wave came back, the launch came too, sliding with it. A lurch, a drop, and suddenly she was off the coral and floating free. Jackie ran to the rail. *Elizabeth* was in deep water, safe for the time being, anyway. But there was a new danger now, because at this stage of the tide the reef was at its most dangerous; almost invisible, a menacing mass just beneath the surface of the rapidly darkening sea. As the water rose further the launch could easily drift back over it. In the coming darkness no rescue craft would dare to follow, and when, eventually, the tide dropped, she'd be stranded, high and dry, surrounded by hectares of coral, another victim of the reef.

Jackie looked for the boy again. He was still there, a diminutive figure, growing smaller and smaller as *Elizabeth* drifted away. She fetched the binoculars from the wheelhouse for a closer look. He had his legs tucked up now as the water swirled around his precarious perch, mere centimetres below his feet.

Suddenly she heard the blast of a hooter, quite close. She spun around, and there, no more than two hundred metres away, was a big Bertram; Lofty Johnson's boat, moving slowly towards her. Through the glasses she could make out her father, standing beside Lofty on the flybridge, and Greg, up the mast, picking a way through the channel. Jackie took the binoculars from her eyes and breathed a long, deep sigh of relief as the game fishing boat inched its way towards her through the gathering gloom.

It was late. The family-room in the private section of Butterfly Island Resort had high ceilings, and the big picture windows were wide open, as always, to catch the breeze, but it was still hot, the churning ceiling fans relentlessly re-circulating the humid air.

Slumped in his favourite chair, Charlie Wilson passed a weary hand across his damp forehead and glanced down at Jackie, sitting at his feet. He was immensely relieved to have her back again. It had been a close call, but he was proud of her; she'd kept her head; not like that crazy kid, charging about all over the reef. They'd had to launch a dinghy to get him off: a devil of a job . . .

'Why do we have to keep him here?' Sally's question brought him back to the here-and-now.

'Because Pat Connolly can't get over till morning.' Connolly was the Sergeant of Police at Ellis River; Charlie had spent some time with him on the two-way, but the policeman hadn't been able to shed any light on the boy. He had no idea who he was, or where he had come from, but in the time honoured fashion, he'd assured Charlie that he would be 'making enquiries'. When pressed, he had patiently explained that this would entail a number of phone calls and that he was not about to dig his colleagues down South out of bed in the middle of the night. Not over a fourteen-year-old kid, who at that moment was safe, and since he was on an island, most decidedly secure. Charlie hadn't been too happy about being landed with the job of jailer, but he'd tried to make the best of it, nailing shutters over the windows of the spare room where they'd put the boy, just to be sure. He'd hated himself as he'd stood back to survey the finished job; he never thought he'd see the day when he'd be locking somebody up on Butterfly Island.

'He wouldn't touch his food.' They all looked up at the announcement to see Mary standing at the door, a worried expression on her normally open, friendly face.

'He'll eat when he gets hungry.' Charlie dismissed the news with an impatient wave, and as the housekeeper came over and sat down he noticed that she was looking very tired, too.

With great effort, Vo Diem had managed to contain his hunger until Mary had left the room, not wishing to give her the satisfaction of watching him eat; but as soon as she'd closed and locked the door behind her he'd been across the room in a flash to the dresser where she'd left the tray. It was Australian food, steak and eggs, but it was the first decent meal he'd had in almost a week, and he had wiped the plate absolutely clean. Now he lay back on the bed replete, in the dark, hands crossed behind his head. The coral cuts and scratches were bothering him; the woman who had brought the food had insisted on spraying his legs with some yellow stuff out of an aerosol can, but they seemed no better; in fact they were really stinging now.

To distract himself from the pain he forced his mind on to something else, listening carefully, analysing the sounds that he could hear outside the room. There was the distant thrubbing of a generator, the occasional rustling of coconut palms, and somewhere in the house, not far away, the muffled ebb and flow of a conversation. He couldn't make out individual words, but he could recognise some of the voices; the man, Charlie, was doing most of the talking, but occasionally he identified the lighter tones of Jackie, the girl who had been his unwitting, and unwilling, passenger that afternoon.

Despite his discomfort, Vo Diem grinned. He'd lay a bet on the subject of the conversation. Him! For a moment he allowed himself to feel grateful to these people who had fed him, tended his wounds, and, most of all, saved his life. They were indeed strange, these Australians; after what he had done they would have been quite justified in leaving him to die out there on the coral reef. He dismissed the thought from his mind at once. Soft nonsense like *that* would only undermine his resolve and distract him from his main purpose, his journey, his quest. He'd be better employed finding something constructive to do.

Diem tried the window. The latch opened easily, but the casement wouldn't move because of the heavy shutters nailed on from the outside, so he moved over to the door, squatting to peer at the lock with an expert eye. The key was still there, so it would be a pushover, but experience told him that *now* was not the time; there was little point in escaping from the room just to walk into someone in the corridor outside. Diem lay down again to wait for the signs of activity in the house to subside, but sleep overtook him before he knew.

He woke with a start, annoyed with himself for drifting off, because now he had lost all track of time. He sat up and listened. The house was still; even the generator was silent now. Then, a shock; through the chinks in the shuttered window he could discern a faint, pale grey glow. Morning!

There wasn't a second to lose. Angry with himself for wasting so much time, he crossed the room carrying a sheet of newspaper that had been used for lining one of the dresser drawers. He slid it under the door until it was projecting into the corridor outside, and then, with a wire coathanger, set to work on the key, jiggling it to and fro with just enough force to make it move.

SPLAT! In the pre-dawn quiet, the sound of metal striking newsprint seemed loud enough to wake the entire house, but it was too late to worry about that now. Vo Diem slid the paper back under the door, and with it came the key.

Out in the corridor he paused only long enough to lock the door again from the outside, and to replace the key; there was no point in advertising his escape; they'd find that out soon enough. A minute later he was out of the house, making his way silently down a sandy path, past little cabins set among groves of coconut palms. He had no idea where he was going, because it had been dark when they had brought him in, but Diem felt confident that he was heading towards the beach. That's where all tracks led, eventually, in a place like this; and a beach meant boats, and boats, as always, meant freedom.

But he was wrong. The path took him to water, but it wasn't the sea. Vo Diem found himself on the edge of a well-kept clearing, in the middle of which was a large swimming pool. As he paused, trying to get his bearings, hundreds of electric bulbs, strung along the fence and through the nearby trees, suddenly glowed, then burst into full brightness, glittering like multi-coloured jewels in the grey dawn. At the same time, somewhere not far away, the generator resumed its familiar, muffled, throbbing roar.

Damn! That meant somebody was up and about.

Cursing himself yet again for wasting the cover of the night-time hours, Diem ran around the pool, down another path on the other side, past more cabins, his feet echoing in his ears like galloping hooves on the hard-packed coral sand. But he didn't care any more: it was too late to worry about making a noise now.

All at once he found himself on the beach; better still, he was looking at a line of canoes, drawn up, inverted, in a neat row on the sand. Salvation! He ran up to the nearest canoe, and had his hands on it, about to turn it over and drag it down to the sea, when he stopped short at the sight of a jagged hole marring the smooth surface of the fibreglass hull. He turned to the next canoe, only to find that it had a hole in it too: same place, same size;

about as big as a man's fist. The next canoe was holed in a similar fashion. Diem moved hurriedly down the line, examining each canoe in turn, but they were all unusable. And then he saw the axe, lying half buried in the sand. They'd all been deliberately smashed! Diem shrugged and turned away; a mystery, but not his problem. He looked around desperately for something else, *anything*, that would float. There was a dinghy further down the beach; his heart leapt, hope renewed; he'd take that instead.

But he never got the chance. Suddenly, two brawny arms grabbed him roughly from behind.

'You flamin' little vandal!' It was Charlie.

Almost by reflex, Diem began to struggle, twisting and kicking in his efforts to wriggle free; but Charlie was a very fit, very angry man, and he merely tightened his grip, making it difficult for Diem to breathe as he was dragged backwards up the beach, his threshing feet leaving a crazy herringbone pattern in the sand.

Jackie came running up, still in her pyjamas.

'See what he's done!' Charlie yelled, but she'd already taken in the scene of destruction in one hurried, horrified glance. Then she looked at Vo Diem; for an instant their eyes met, but he knew what she was thinking, and just as quickly looked away.

Charlie spoke again, softly now, with his mouth only centimetres from the boy's ear. 'I'll see they lock you up for this!' Vo Diem recognised the quiet menace in his voice; it wasn't a threat, it was a promise!

Sergeant Pat Connolly edged the police launch towards the Butterfly Island jetty, threw the engine into reverse to check the speed, switched off, then came out of the cabin to toss Jackie a line. He was an imposing figure; a big man, with a ruddy, weather-beaten complexion, white moustache, and a ready smile that lit up his whole face. His stature was further enhanced by his uniform;

dark blue trousers, a pale blue, open-necked shirt with the triple chevron of his rank and the brightly-coloured insignia of the Queensland Police emblazoned upon each sleeve; the lot surmounted by a broad-brimmed, khaki bush hat.

'You took your time getting here,' Charlie said. Connolly ignored the rebuke. An amiable man, he could see the lighter side of what to him so far appeared to be a boyish prank; irresponsible, illegal, but a prank, nevertheless.

'I nearly brought reinforcements,' he grinned. 'Can't take risks with a dangerous criminal.' He chuckled at his own joke but Charlie didn't even crack a smile. 'What's up?' asked Connolly. 'Lost your sense of humour?'

'Yeah.'

The policeman soon understood why. Offending axe in hand, Charlie stood beside him as he surveyed the row of wrecked canoes. 'What's up, Pat? Out of jokes?' he asked. The sergeant nodded. It wasn't a laughing matter any more.

'The little vandal! I'm sorry, Charlie.'

Charlie dismissed the apology with a shrug. 'It's money I haven't got, Pat,' he said. 'Just get that kid off my island as soon as you can.'

But Sergeant Connolly wanted to talk to Vo Diem first; police procedure demanded it, and he was a stickler for regulations. They went together to the spare room, where the sergeant knelt beside the bed and spoke slowly, deliberately, and not unkindly to Vo Diem, trying every trick in the book to get through.

'I . . . am . . . Sergeant . . . Connolly. Who . . . are . . . you?' he asked, for the umpteenth time; but there was no response.

Connolly climbed stiffly to his feet, his patience worn paper thin. He stood towering over Diem, irritably scratching the back of his head. 'Look son,' he growled, 'you're in big enough trouble as it is. Carry on like this and you'll make things worse for yourself.'

'What's the point, Pat?' interrupted Charlie. 'He can't speak English.'

'Let me handle it, will you, Charlie,' grunted Connolly, peeved.

A wide-eyed Greg had been watching proceedings with great interest; this was the first time he'd seen an actual police interrogation. 'Are you going to put him in jail, Sergeant?' he asked, carried away by the excitement of it all. Connolly bristled and Charlie glared, but the situation was saved by the appearance of Jackie at the door.

'Mary wants to know if Sergeant Connolly's going to have a cuppa' before he leaves, Dad.' The question was addressed to Charlie, but the policeman replied, his face softening at once.

'The answer is yes, love.'

As they all filed from the room she lingered in the doorway, fascinated, gazing at Vo Diem as he sat impassively on the bed. In the corridor, Charlie turned to Greg. 'Keep that door locked, and stay outside.'

'You're not taking any chances,' observed Connolly.

'You haven't seen that kid in action,' Charlie replied, and both men trooped off down the corridor towards their cups of tea, and Mary's scones, leaving a self-important Greg behind to push the fascinated Jackie out of the way so that he could close the door. 'The Sarge's going to lock him up,' he announced as he turned the key.

'They don't lock kids up,' Jackie retorted.

'That's what you think,' Greg said. He wanted his sister to agree with him, but she stayed silent. The notion of being shut away worried her, and she didn't want to think about it. After a pause, Greg tried again 'Well, don't you think he deserves it?'

Still no reply.

'Those canoes'll cost Dad thousands of bucks!' per-
sisted Greg, still trying to provoke a response.

'I know that,' she replied evenly, but her mind was on
reasons, not rights and wrongs. 'But if he was trying to
escape, why did he waste time smashing our canoes?'

As soon as Vo Diem saw the waiting police launch, he
stopped in his tracks, a surge of panic welling up inside.
He'd watched people being loaded on to police boats in
Vietnam; and they'd never been seen again. He felt a
hand on his shoulder. Connolly was standing there,
close behind. The sergeant nodded towards the boat,
and when Diem still hesitated, the grip tightened, not
painfully, but just enough to indicate that he was
expected to walk on.

But he didn't. He stood there, his feet anchored to the
wooden planking by fear. As far as he was concerned,
this was it; the beginning of the end. Connolly's jaw
hardened. 'You've got to come with me, son,' he said, as
kindly as he could. 'Don't make it more difficult for
yourself.' Diem felt himself being propelled gently but
firmly along the deck; he had no choice but to go, and
when the policeman indicated where he should sit on
board the launch he obeyed without further resistance.
As Connolly got the vessel under way he caught a final
glimpse of Charlie, standing on the jetty, waving to the
policeman, no doubt very relieved to see them go.

The trip back to the mainland gave Vo Diem breathing space; time to think. He was nothing if not resilient,
a survivor from way back, and by the time the launch
entered the mouth of the Ellis River he had begun to
gather together the remnants of his shattered morale.
All was not lost, he kept telling himself; he wasn't in jail
yet. All he wanted was another opportunity; if one
didn't present itself he'd *make* something happen; and
as the launch came alongside the wharf Diem's eyes
were everywhere, looking for another lucky break.

Diem expected to be whisked away into the bush, to some isolated barbed wire enclosure with its contingent of dispirited prisoners slowly broiling under the tropic sun, but instead the police car turned into a tree-lined, flower-bedecked street, bustling with casually-dressed Australians, hurrying to get their shopping done before it rained. The boy recognised the big Coke sign, and sighed. He was back where he'd started yesterday. The sergeant eased the vehicle into the kerb in front of Harry Wong's Chinese Takeaway, switched off, and swivelled around in his seat.

'Now,' he said, 'let's see if we can find someone who speaks your language.'

But Vo Diem made no move to get out. He reached instead for the policeman's heavy storm jacket, which was lying in a crumpled heap on the seat beside him, then lay back full length, and pulled it up so that it covered him completely, head to foot. Connolly frowned. 'Have it your own way, mate,' he said, and eased his big frame out of the car, slammed the door, and went into the café, leaving the Vietnamese boy behind.

A few minutes later he was back, accompanied by a cheerful little man wearing thick-soled rubber sandals and a grubby white apron over an open-necked shirt and baggy shorts: Harry Wong, who wasn't too happy about being dragged away from his preparations for the lunch-time rush.

'Fair go, Sarge!' he protested. 'I'm up to me ears in curried prawns!' Harry looked Chinese, but his accent was as Australian as damper and billy tea.

'Just try to communicate with him, that's all I ask,' pleaded Connolly.

'You know how many different Asian languages there are, Sarge?' asked Harry. 'Let alone dialects and accents? I only speak a bit of Cantonese, and I learnt most of that off menus.'

The policeman grinned at his frankness. 'I want his

name, and where he's from, that's all,' he said, reaching down to open the rear door. 'Give it a go, Harry, please.' The Chinaman shrugged, bent down and fired off a burst of heavily Australian-accented Cantonese.

'What's your name boy?' he asked. There was no reply. Harry pulled his head out of the doorway. 'I don't think I'm getting through to him, Sarge,' he said, with a half-embarrassed, half-amused grin.

Connolly's brow furrowed; he sensed that something was amiss at once, and reached a long arm past his would-be interpreter to jerk the storm jacket off the seat. But all he saw was bare upholstery; there was nobody underneath it now.

'The cheeky little . . . !' He straightened up to his full height and looked quickly up and down the busy street, but the boy was long gone, vanished into the crowd.

An hour later Diem was back at Ellis River Airport, in his hiding place beside the hangar. Taking extra care not to be discovered, he carefully studied a large, twin-engined plane that was standing on the tarmac about twenty metres away. It was obviously being readied for departure, because he'd just seen a petrol tanker driving off, and now two men were taking boxes from a trailer and loading them through the large doorway near the tail. Diem didn't know much about planes. Even though the skies had been constantly full of them back in Vietnam, he'd seldom seen one up close; they didn't take kindly to kids hanging around military airfields in a war zone. Apart from the big jet that had brought him to Australia from the refugee camp, he'd never actually had a ride in one in his life. But he'd now decided that flying was the best way to cover a lot of ground in the shortest possible time, and he knew that he had a long, long way to go. But was this particular plane travelling in the right direction? Then he made a decision. Who cared *where* it was going? He had to get away; things were rapidly getting too hot for him here!

The men completed their loading, climbed aboard a little tractor and towed the empty trailer away. Diem tensed; for the first time since he'd been watching, there was nobody around. It was now or never. Sensing that familiar thrill of excitement, he took a deep breath, left his cover, and ran. The twenty metres seemed twenty kilometres, but he finally arived at the plane, and paused at the foot of the stairs, unsure. There was only one door; one way in, one way out. Once on board, what if there was nowhere to hide? He'd be trapped. There must be someplace else. But where? In desperation he ran under the wing and crouched behind one of the big tyres, which provided temporary shelter while he tried to collect his thoughts.

Then, as he crouched there, feeling vulnerable and exposed, he found the perfect spot, right above his head; a cavernous hole from which projected the massive struts supporting the wheels. Diem glanced back towards the hangar. The coast was still clear, so he climbed nimbly up the undercarriage, and squeezed into the hole, twisting his body uncomfortably to fit into the awkward, confined space.

He didn't have long to wait. He heard voices, followed by the trundling of the steps being wheeled away; then the door slammed, a starter whined very close above his head, the engine fired, coughed, then burst into a deafening roar, making his ears ring. Diem renewed his precarious grip, wedging himself in as securely as he could, and peered down to watch the tarmac slide by as the wheel began to turn.

It was a rough ride to the end of the runway; several times Diem felt himself about to fall, and to make matters worse, the rapidly-heating engine began to make his aluminium cell uncomfortably warm. Vo Diem gritted his teeth; if it was like this on the ground, what would it be like up in the air? But it was too late to get out now; all he could do was close his eyes, hang on, and hope.

The plane lurched, and he felt, rather than heard the engine note rise to a new crescendo, way past the threshold of pain; a mind-bending, excrutiating, unearthly roar: there was a tremendous surge of power, and he sneaked a glance at the black streaks on the concrete runway sliding past beneath him, faster, faster, faster, until they were a blur. Diem snapped his eyes shut again and hung on for dear life.

Suddenly the vibrations eased. He was still painfully enveloped in noise, but he wasn't being buffeted around any more, so he risked another look.

They were in the air! The runway was a long way below now, moving past more slowly. And then he became aware of something else; the wheel, hanging suspended in space, still spinning after the dash down the runway, was moving upwards. The struts supporting it telescoped and began to fold, bringing it up towards him.

It was going to come into his refuge!

He shrank back, trying to flatten himself against the hot aluminium wall. The wheel came closer. He screamed, but his voice was lost in the engine's roar as the gigantic black tyre rose whirling into his precarious retreat, obliterating everything else from view.

THREE

Charlie Wilson lingered on the jetty for some time after the launch bearing the policeman and his reluctant passenger had disappeared into the morning haze. He was deep in thought. The kid had left the island, but his involvement with the fugitive boy was far from over, he knew that in his bones. For a start, Pat Connolly had asked him to lay official charges, necessitating another trip across to Ellis River; later he'd probably have to appear in court: a lot of time wasted; all because the young idiot had taken it into his head to pinch his boat. Then there was the matter of the smashed canoes; goodness knows where he could find the money to have them repaired. He might manage it himself, he supposed, with young Greg's help, but that would take more time, and meanwhile he had a resort to run.

Depressed, he leant against the wooden railing of the jetty, and gazed down through the clear water at the thousands of tiny fish massing around the barnacle-encrusted concrete piles. Occasionally there was the silver flash of an individual but mostly the whole shoal would move as one, darting into the shadows to escape some danger, imaginary or real, and then, as if directed by some mass consciousness, drifting cautiously out into sunlit water once again. Charlie's eye ran up a pile, out of the water, along the sun-bleached timbers of the jetty, and came to rest on two rusty railway lines that were mounted on the rough-hewn wooden planking at his feet. He smiled to himself: he remembered his father laying that track, so that they could carry heavy supplies ashore from the launch. The rails and the little wagon that ran on them were still in daily use: not bad after almost thirty years.

He turned away from the sea and looked back along the rails. The planking of the jetty gave way to a sandy path that meandered between a cluster of coconut palms and she-oaks that cast cool patterns of dappled shadow on the white coral sand. On each side of the jetty was a long curve of gently-sloping beach, beyond that were the buildings, beckoning through the trees. Butterfly Island Resort. His resort; and as always, Charlie surrendered to its spell. Suddenly, depressed no more, he set off, whistling, towards the house.

He found the girls with Mary in the family-room. 'Are you still going across to Ellis River this afternoon?' he asked Sally. She was cutting something out of a newspaper, but stopped at once at the sound of his voice.

'Yes, Dad,' she replied, indicating a folder lying on the table. 'Finalising the printing of the brochures. Ready to go.' There was something odd about her manner; she seemed excited about something, and Charlie thought he could also detect an element of guilt in those wide-open brown eyes. He shrugged to himself; with teenage daughters, you could never tell.

He transferred his attention to Jackie, and glanced at his watch. 'Ten minutes to school,' he reminded her. Like Greg, she took her lessons by correspondence, supplemented by regular sessions on School of the Air, talking by two-way radio with her teacher whom she only met when she travelled the two hundred and fifty kilometres to the school sports in Cairns, once a year. 'And I'd like you to find a bit of time to tidy up the garden, Jackie,' he said, on his way out. Jackie needed reminding about her chores once in a while.

'Yes. The tourists are going to flock here to look at the garden, Jackie.' The sarcasm in Sally's voice stopped Charlie at the door.

'What's wrong with *you*?' he asked.

She shrugged. 'Just thinking out loud, Dad.'

That wasn't good enough. Something was troubling her; and it was time she told him what was on her mind. He turned and came back into the room. 'Come on, out with it,' he said.

Sally paused. She knew her father. She'd started something and he'd make sure she finished it now. She took a deep breath and withdrew a crumpled piece of paper out of the folder. 'The Pattersons have cancelled!' she said, holding it up.

Charlie shrugged. 'So? You've been reading the mail.'

'Is *that* all you can say, Dad?' blurted Sally, shaking her head in disbelief. 'The Pattersons have been coming to Butterfly for years, and now they're going to *Reef Royale*!' She tossed the letter down in front of her father as if the name of the big resort were a dirty word.

Charlie left the paper where it lay. 'We can't compete with Reef Royale,' he said. 'We're not even going to try! Butterfly's natural and unspoiled, and if the Pattersons can't see what we've got here then I'm sorry for them. Sure, we need to upgrade a few facilities, but this place is never going to be like your big hotel chain. I mean, if you like that kind of thing, why leave the city when you go on holiday?'

One glance at Sally told him that his explanation had gone over like a lead balloon.

'I think the Pattersons are right,' she said.

Charlie was surprised. 'Oh, you do, eh?' he said.

'Yes I do.'

'Well, go on; tell me why,' he challenged.

'OK, Dad, I will. I'll give you one example. I'm supposed to be Entertainments Officer around here, right?' Sally was getting into her stride now.

Charlie nodded. 'Right.'

She lifted her arms in exasperation. 'But how can I be, when we don't have anything that you could call entertainment?'

Charlie shrugged. 'Simple pleasures, Sally! That's what makes this island different. Novelty nights, bushwalks, campfire singalongs . . .'

'*Singalongs*!' Sally interrupted him with a short, impatient laugh. 'Oh yeah! You should've seen the way the kids looked at me last year when I said we were going to have a *singalong*. The Patterson kids, by the way!'

'What's wrong with a singalong?' Charlie was stung by her outburst; singalongs were very dear to his heart: he remembered many a pleasant evening spent around a fire on the beach as a boy.

She explained it to him, patiently. 'It's all right, Dad, if you're a hundred years old. Listen to me. I've had a great idea. It'll make us a lot of money, too.'

'I'm listening.' His arms were still folded across his chest.

'A rock concert, Dad. We invite bands from all over the country. A four-day rock concert. We'd get thousands of kids, paying customers. They can camp all over the island. We can put a stage on the beach, with speakers to blast the music. They'll hear it on the mainland. It'll be fantastic!'

Charlie was speechless with shock, his mouth gaping, his head moving slowly from side to side. This couldn't be his daughter speaking! But the horrible truth sank in; it was, and she was still talking. 'It'd only be for four days,' she went on, eyes bright with enthusiasm. 'It wouldn't hurt the island much, and it'd pay for everything you want to do!'

He smiled grimly at her. 'Eight out of ten for trying, Sal.' He made a move for the door, but Sally wasn't about to let him go without firing a parting shot.

She called out after him, 'You're going to have to compromise, sooner or later!'

'The expression on his face! I wish I'd had a camera!' Mary chuckled, but Sally refused to see the funny side. She spoke through her teeth with frustration.

'He knocks back every idea I come up with!'

Mary smiled sympathetically. 'Well, don't give up. Your dad counts on you. If you want my advice. . . .'

But Sally didn't. She interrupted savagely, eyes ablaze. 'Mary, this is between Dad and me!' Then she swept up the folder and was gone.

Momentarily shocked, then hurt, but not offended, Mary let her go. Sally was right. She'd gone too far, said too much; she was not a member of the Wilson family; she was merely the housekeeper, the paid help. The trouble was, she so often ached to be much more.

It was an unpleasant trip across to the mainland. Sally stayed on deck, out of her father's way, for most of the journey, and that suited them both. As far as Charlie was concerned, grievances had been aired, and that was the end of the matter. If people wanted to go to Reef Royale, or Surfers' Paradise, or Timbuktu, for that matter, there was little he could do to stop them. As for Sally's madcap scheme . . . well, there'd be no rock concerts on Butterfly; he'd made that abundantly clear.

Sally had other reasons for keeping to herself. Her silence didn't signify acceptance of her father's edict; far from it. She had said how she felt, to no avail, and now the time for *talking* was past. Now there were things that she had to *do*.

Pat Connolly was waiting on the marina, and Charlie moved to the rail to greet him as Sally made fast. 'I'm sorry to have to tell you this, mate,' the policeman said, his face red, 'but you might as well go home again. The kid's gone.'

'Gone?' Charlie was surprised, then annoyed, then

amused. It wasn't often that you saw Pat Connolly embarrassed, and he fought to suppress a grin.

'I'm glad you think it's funny!' said the Sergeant, colouring more.

'Me? Never!' Charlie had lost the battle and was now grinning from ear to ear.

'He'd been as good as gold,' moaned Connolly. 'I only left him in the car for a minute . . .'

'You're lucky he didn't steal that, too,' interrupted Charlie. 'Have you searched for him?' As Connolly nodded wearily, wiping his brow, Charlie suddenly remembered the policeman's sarcastic remarks earlier in the day. Now he was going to pay him back, with interest. His grin widened: 'Maybe you need reinforcements,' he said.

Sally came out of the wheelhouse, folder in hand. 'See you back here in a hour, Sal,' her father grinned, still enjoying the joke. She smiled briefly but didn't say anything; she didn't like deceiving him, but she had other plans.

She walked to the printers, and gave them the details for the brochure, and then took one of Ellis River's few taxis out to the airport. Bob Gallio, about to board Gallio-Air's one and only DC-3, stopped and waited as she ran across the tarmac towards him. 'Where did you spring from?' he asked, pleasantly surprised, but she didn't bother him with details.

'Are you still going to Charters Towers today?' she asked.

He nodded. 'We're just about to take off. Why?'

'Can I come with you?'

For a moment Bob was thrown. 'Sure,' he replied, puzzled. 'But this isn't your day off.'

'It's business, Bob.' Sally said excitedly. 'Big enough to get Dad out of debt.'

'Now I'm curious,' he grinned, as they walked together towards the plane.

In the cockpit, Rick, the captain, a man in his mid-twenties, was waiting to begin the pre-flight check. 'Got a passenger, mate,' said Bob as he slipped into the right-hand seat.

Rick smiled. 'G'day, Sal. This is a pleasant surprise.'

'She's got some business to do in Charters Towers,' said Bob, by way of explanation.

'I bet,' said Rick, with a knowing smile. As captain of the aircraft, he had the final say about the carrying of unofficial passengers, and he was acutely aware of Bob sitting anxiously beside him, waiting for a final 'yes' or 'no'. He thought quickly. It was strictly against company policy, but these were nice kids, out for a bit of harmless fun. What the heck! 'No worries,' he said, 'it's not as though we have to write a ticket or anything.' He looked Bob straight in the eye, well aware that he was the boss's son. 'Your old man will never know.'

They were busy for a while then, starting the engines and taking off, and Sally knew enough about Bob's work to leave him alone. When they were in the air, climbing steadily towards the south, she reached forward and tapped him on the shoulder, showing him the item that she'd clipped from the newspaper that morning.

Bob read it through. It was a story about a country singer, and he could make no sense of it at all. He handed it back. 'So, Snowy Rivers has had his southern tour cancelled. So what?'

'Snowy's manager is stuck in Charters Towers until tomorrow,' Sally replied, raising her voice above the drone of the engines. 'And I've got an appointment to see him!'

'You've gotta be kidding!' Amazed, Bob turned around in his seat.

'No. I talked to him on the phone this morning,' she blurted, very enthusiastic now. 'A Mr Jacobs. If I can get a big country and western star like Snowy Rivers to do a week on Butterfly, we'll pack the place all summer!'

Bob shook his head sceptically. 'I don't believe this,' he said. 'Do you know what you'd have to pay for Snowy Rivers? For crying out loud, Sally, Butterfly Island doesn't even have a *band*!'

Sally smiled at his lack of vision. 'If I sign him,' she said evenly, 'we'll soon *get* a band.'

'You're not old enough to sign anything!' he retorted.

For a moment she was taken aback: she hadn't thought of that. 'Well, I'll try bluff,' she said. Suddenly she was angry; everyone seemed to do nothing but place obstacles and objections in her way. 'I've got to try *something*, Bob!' she snapped.

He shook his head. He couldn't understand what Charlie was doing, sending Sally on a wild goose chase like this. Then, suddenly, realisation dawned. 'Your father doesn't know about this, does he?'

She smiled ruefully. 'He does by now. I left a note in the wheelhouse!'

The DC-3 droned on over the vastness of North Queensland. The lushness of the coastal plains was left far behind, and now the parched interior stretched out on either side, as far as the eye could see; brown, open, generally flat country, sprinkled with scrubby trees. There wasn't much sign of life; no major roads, a few, ill-defined tracks. Occasionally a homestead with its collection of outbuildings would appear ahead, move steadily closer, and then slide by until it was out of sight behind the wing, and then there would be nothing again; no evidence of human habitation; reminding Sally that they were flying over country that was largely still untamed, one of Earth's last frontiers. Not a place in which to be forced down.

To take her mind off that remote possibility, she studied the ground closely. The trees were more prolific along the edges of the few rivers, marking their courses with two parallel, snaking lines of drab olive green.

From directly overhead, she could easily see that there wasn't much water in the rivers now; just yellow sand bars, with the very occasional gleam of a lagoon, for this was the end of the dry season. The whole country breathlessly awaited the monsoon, that seasonal inrush of air that brought life-giving rain, but Sally knew that with the rain would come destructive cyclones and floods, for this was a place of nature's extremes. The scene below would be vastly different then, the plains inundated from horizon to horizon as the swollen rivers overflowed. At such times, flying near the coast, it was sometimes difficult to detect where the land ended and the sea began.

Her train of thought was interrupted by a short, sharp shock that jolted the whole structure of the plane. She tensed, but almost as soon as it began, the vibration was gone, and all she was aware of once more was the easy movement through the air accompanied by the soothing drone of the engines. She glanced at Rick and Bob. From her position in the jump seat, behind them, she couldn't see their faces, but they seemed quite relaxed. Situation normal. Sally leant back, closed her eyes, and tried to relax, too.

There it was again! A violent jolt, as if someone were hitting the plane with a big hammer; once, twice, three times; then it was gone. Sally sat bolt upright, eyes wide, white knuckles and sweaty palms threatening to squeeze right through the arm of her seat. She watched for a reaction from Rick and Bob; they *must* have felt *that*!

They had. Both were sitting forward now, eyes scanning the instruments, searching for signs of trouble. When the next shock came, longer and more violent than the others, Sally's mouth went dry, and she felt an icy-cold emptiness spreading rapidly deep down inside. All thoughts of her meeting with Mr Jacobs, and the Snowy Rivers concert, were long gone; she had other things on her mind. Her heart began to race, and with it, her imagination. They were going to crash. In the middle of nowhere. Even if they survived, they wouldn't be found for weeks. Perhaps never. Flying was ridiculous. It was unnatural. Dangerous. She should never have come.

Bob turned around and gave her a reassuring smile, 'We're having a bit of trouble with Number Two,' he said, jerking a thumb at the engine in question, but all Sally could manage in return was a weak grin. She tightened her grip on the seat. They were thousands of metres up in the air, in an ancient collection of nuts and bolts that was about to shake itself to pieces! *A bit of trouble*! That would have to be the understatement of the year! Bob went on, explaining the technicalities, but she was only half listening. She was frightened, all she wanted was to feel her two feet safely back on solid ground.

And then, the engine began to misfire again. Bob started to point out the symptoms on the instrument panel, but Sally didn't need a quivering needle to tell her that something was *drastically* wrong now; the vibration didn't go away, and it was more violent than before, setting up a harsh, unpleasant, irregular beat that threatened to pop every rivet out of the ancient airframe.

'Time to feather it, I think.' Even as he spoke, Rick's hands were moving over the controls in a practised, unhurried drill, and as Sally watched, the propeller of the right hand engine slowed, then stopped, and suddenly the jarring sensation had disappeared and they were droning peacefully through the sky as if nothing had ever been wrong.

'We'll check it out when we get to Baxter's place,' said Rick. 'We're only about fifteen minutes out.'

'Happens all the time,' said Bob, with an apologetic grin. She nodded, then closed her eyes, praying that they'd get to Baxter's before it happened to the other engine, too.

They landed safely on the dirt airstrip, throwing up a huge cloud of dust, turned, and taxied back in zig-zag fashion, because with only one power-plant it was impossible for Rick to steer a straight path. The propeller on the good engine jerked to a stop, and in the welcome silence, Sally breathed a sigh of relief.

'You can let go now,' Bob laughed, and looking down she suddenly realised that she still had a vicelike grip on her seat! Embarrassed, she let go and unbuckled her belt. Then she made her way down the sloping floor towards the big door, swung it open, and jumped down, grateful for the feel of solid earth once more.

Sally's immediate impression was of sky; a big, pale, overpowering, almost white-hot sky, with a couple of wedgetail eagles describing lazy circles high above. The country was flat and featureless, stretching to a shimmering horizon. There were few trees; just clumps of long, coarse, dry grass, sprouting in tufts like the bristles of some gigantic scrubbing brush. The dessicated ground felt hot to walk on, even through the thick rubber soles of her sandals.

The plane had stopped beside Baxter's 'terminal'; a ramshackle structure made out of bush timber: four poles at each corner, with a rusty galvanised iron roof: just enough to provide some shade from the fierce sun. Of Baxter himself there was no sign. Sally looked back at the plane. Rick and Bob were removing the cowling from the offending engine, but there seemed little she could do to help, so she strolled over into the shade of the wing. She looked up, then stiffened, unable to believe her eyes.

'Bob!' He heard her anguished cry, ran over, and following her shaking, outstretched arm he saw it, too: a small brown arm, hanging limply from beneath the wing.

It took them several minutes to extricate Vo Diem from the wheel well and lower him gently to the ground, taking great care not to let him fall. As they laid his unconscious figure on a blanket in the shadow of the wing a four-wheel drive skidded to a dusty halt beside the plane.

'What's this?' asked Jerry Baxter, hurrying across. He was in his late sixties; tall, thin, and toughened by a lifetime in the bush; fitter than a lot of men half his age. He'd heard the DC-3 fly over, but his homestead was a good five kilometres from the airstrip.

Bob looked up. 'A stowaway, Mr Baxter. The crazy kid was hiding in the wheel well. He's lucky to be alive.'

Sally finished taking the boy's pulse, then bent over so that her cheek was close to his nose, paused for a moment, then looked up at Bob. 'He's hardly breathing,' she said, her face grim. 'And I don't know about that lump on his head. We've got to get him to a doctor.'

Bob glanced up at Rick, on the wing, struggling with the engine cowling in the full heat of the sun. 'How does it look, mate?' he called.

The pilot wiped the sweat from his brow with a greasy hand. 'It's going to need some work,' he replied. 'Couple of hours at least.'

That was too long.

'There's the bush hospital,' the grazier suggested. 'About fifty miles down the track.'

'Could we borrow your truck?' asked Sally.

'Go for your life.' Baxter answered without hesitation in the true tradition of the North, then bent to help Bob lift the inert form from the ground.

The four-wheel drive jolted along through the bush, Bob spinning the wheel furiously to stay on the track as it curved around giant anthills, dropped without warning into gullies and washouts, and skirted half-hidden, burnt-out stumps, fallen logs and trees. Sally was in the back, cradling the boy's head. 'Can't you go any faster?' she called.

'I'm doing my best. It's a rotten road,' replied Bob, but he trod a little harder on the accelerator just the same, cautiously increasing speed.

Sally was worried; although the boy felt cold and clammy, he was sweating profusely, and from time to time she used a handkerchief to gently mop his brow. From her rudimentary knowledge of first aid she could identify the symptoms of shock and exposure; his foot had been caught in the wheel well and was probably broken; almost certainly sprained; and heaven alone knew what other internal injuries he had sustained during the flight.

Suddenly there was a violent jolt as the Landcruiser hit a particularly severe bump, almost jerking the boy's head from her protective arms. 'Slow down a bit!' she yelled.

'You said go fast!' Bob argued, without slackening speed.

'It's too bumpy, Bob!' protested Sally. He's in shock! Slow down!' Bob shook his head and eased his foot off the pedal. You never knew what women *really* wanted you to do!

Then, without warning, the steering wheel was almost wrested from his hands by some unseen force that was turning the vehicle irresistibly to the right. Bob knew that feeling; he'd experienced it many times before, with his father's four-wheel drive.

'What's the matter?' asked Sally.

'We've got a flat tyre,' he replied, pulling up. He climbed out and hurried to the back of the truck to check the spare; then rummaged around looking for a jack. Sally was really worried now; the boy seemed to be having difficulty in breathing; his lips and fingernails were blue. It was a good thing that they'd thought to bring an oxygen bottle from the plane. She opened the valve, held the mask over his face, and was relieved to see his colour return as the life-giving gas had an almost immediate effect. Now all she could do was wait. Bob was struggling to change the tyre and she heard him curse as he barked his knuckles in his haste, but finally the job was done.

'Nearly there,' he called, slinging the damaged tyre into the back of the truck. He slipped behind the wheel, started the engine, engaged the gears and, well-shod once more, the Landcruiser lurched away down the track.

The bush hospital was about the size of a small house, very neat, made of timber weatherboards, with a steep, corrugated iron roof and wide, shady verandahs all round. It had just five beds. There was no doctor, but the staff of two highly-experienced resident sisters were well-versed in the ways of bushmen and the treatment of outback ills. The Flying Doctor made regular clinic visits from his base in Cairns, and could always be consulted by radio if required. In emergencies, patients could be flown out from Baxter's, but it was a long, bumpy ride to the airstrip; Sally and Bob could vouch for that!

They were waiting on the verandah now, and turned anxiously as the screen door opened and Sister came out; a capable-looking, no-nonsense woman in her late twenties wearing a crisp white uniform and sensible shoes. 'He'll be OK,' she smiled. 'He's suffering from shock and exposure, and a sprained ankle. Nothing more.'

Sally was relieved. 'I thought he was going to die.' she said.

'It's nothing short of a miracle that he's alive,' the sister said, her voice taking on that formidable, authoritative tone that nurses often have. 'Such a stupid, dangerous thing to do!'

'How long will he have to stay, Sister?' Bob asked respectfully.

'He should be right by morning,' she smiled. She took her leave, gently closing the screen door. Sally leant against Bob, glad to feel his comforting arm around her, then looked up, concerned by a faraway look in his eyes.

'You look worried, Bob,' she said softly, and then suddenly she remembered why: Sergio would know all about it now. Poor Bob; he'd be in big trouble over this trip. 'You're not mad with me, are you?' she asked, snuggling up.

Bob laughed. 'Who? Me? No! *Your* father's going to kill me; *my* father's going to kill me. He cuddled her closer, looked down, and smiled. 'Why should I be mad with *you*?'

Next day, they brought Vo Diem back to Ellis River. Pat Connolly met the Gallio-Air plane, and this time the Sergeant was taking no chances: a constable sat in the back of the police car beside the fugitive during the short drive into town, and at the station Connolly closed the cell door with a clang and turned the key with some satisfaction. He wasn't going to be caught with egg foo-yong on his face again!

'What happens now, Pat?' asked Charlie. He and Jackie had picked up Sally from the same flight and had followed the police car into town.

'Well, I've got a bit of information on him,' said Pat. 'It seems he came to Australia about eight months ago; migrated to join relatives in Brisbane. He's Vietnamese; apparently he was one of the boat people. Lost his parents at sea.'

Jackie was stunned. A wave of pity swept over her as she looked at the boy, pale and dispirited, sitting stoically behind the bars of the cell. 'Where does he go from here?' asked Charlie, taken back by the news, too.

'Seeing as how he stole your boat and vandalised

your property, he'll be charged and sent before the juvenile court,' replied the Sergeant, using his official voice. 'And then,' he continued in a softer tone, 'I'll have to send him to Taboundi.'

'Taboundi . . . that's the Youth Remand Centre, isn't it?' Jackie heard her father ask.

Connolly nodded. 'Yeah. A shame, isn't it, considering the rough time the kid's already had.' He held up a clipboard to which a typed sheet had been attached. 'Oh well,' he sighed, 'better sign your statement, Charlie. Just here. . . .' He indicated the place with a pen.

Charlie took the clipboard and read the statement through. 'What's this?' he asked. 'Vo Diem?'

'That's his name,' said Connolly.

Charlie looked at the boy, then at Jackie, then at Connolly, then back at the boy. 'Vo Diem,' he said again, more to himself than anyone else.'

'Just sign there, Charlie,' said the Sergeant.

Charlie shook his head. 'Forget it, Pat,' he said. 'The kid's been through enough without me having a go at him as well.' Connolly shrugged. He'd expected as much; he knew Charlie Wilson pretty well. Charlie nodded his goodbye and moved off, followed by Sally, but Jackie stayed.

'Jackie!' Sally called. She obeyed, giving Vo Diem one last, lingering look.

Outside nobody said much as the three of them made their way down the main street, but curiosity finally got the better of Jackie. 'Did you really save that boy's . . . Vo Diem's . . . life?' she asked, having difficulty as she tried to pronounce his name for the first time.

'That's what they said at the hospital,' Sally smiled, then glanced across at her father. 'I'm glad I did that first-aid course, Dad,' she said.

Charlie nodded agreement. 'It was a smarter move than going on that plane!' Sally managed a smile; her father would have a lot more to say on that subject later on, of that she was sure.

They reached an intersection, and Charlie paused. 'The brochures should be ready,' he said. 'You go and pick them up and we'll wait for you at the wharf.'

'Yes, Dad,' said Sally, obediently, moving off, and this time she intended to make the rendezvous!

Jackie listened to the ropes creak as *Elizabeth* pulled lazily at her moorings, and breathed in deeply, filling her lungs with the bracing tang of ships and the sea. She gazed out across the sparkling river, past the sprinkling of white gulls that bobbed on the wavelets at her feet, past the green curtain of mangroves on the opposite bank, past the distant, cloud-wreathed mountains, rising steeply on the other side of the coastal plain: her thoughts were still on the boy. 'Why would the Sergeant send Vo Diem to Taboundi?' she asked, getting the name right this time.

Charlie shrugged. 'That's the way the law is,' he said.

'What's it like, Dad?'

'Taboundi?' Charlie scratched his chin and thought. 'I wouldn't want to see any of you end up there, put it that way,' he said finally.

'Then why is the Sergeant sending him there?' she asked again.

'You can't keep a child in police cells, Jackie,' replied Charlie. 'Pat doesn't have any choice.'

'Suppose he did have?' she said. He looked at her but she avoided his gaze and went on, as if thinking aloud, 'Somewhere the boy couldn't possibly get away from.' She looked at her father now; straight in the eye, and said, softly, 'Somewhere like an island.'

'You must think I'm soft in the head!' Charlie snorted. He'd been expecting that.

Jackie didn't say anything more for a while; the only sounds were the little slaps of the wavelets on *Elizabeth's* hull, the creaking of the ropes and the occasional screech of a squabbling seagull. Finally she spoke again. 'Why do the boat people come here?' she asked.

Charlie didn't have a ready answer. 'Looking for a better life, I suppose . . . freedom . . . some place where they've got a chance.' She was getting to him and he didn't like it. 'Look,' he burst out, 'you don't have to *try* to make me feel sorry for him, Jackie. I already *am*! But what you want is just plain *crazy*!'

'It'd only be for twenty-four hours!' she countered. The time for a soft-sell approach was past.

'Time enough for him to wreck the rest of the island?' Charlie said.

'I bet he feels bad about what he did, and he knows that Sally saved his life!' Jackie argued.

'Maybe,' Charlie conceded, 'but it's not as simple as bringing a stray cat home.'

'I know that, Dad,' she said, pausing to let it simmer for a while.

'We've got enough problems of our own!' blurted Charlie, but she didn't respond. She knew that he was arguing with himself, now.

'He doesn't speak English,' he went on. 'How would we communicate with him?'

'Dad, he hasn't got a *mother*.' Jackie said.

'Pat Connolly would never agree to it,' he countered, grasping at straws. She remained silent.

'Well,' he said, finally, 'I s'pose there's no harm in *asking*.' Jackie threw her arms around his neck. Sometimes her father made her very proud!

FOUR

Greg Wilson heaved the anchor over the side of the workboat with a splash, then stood back to watch the nylon rope buzz over the edge of the aluminium gunwale with a sharp sound like fingers running down the teeth of a comb. He looked back along the still-foaming wake to Butterfly Island, three kilometres away. If he squinted he could make out the jetty, poking like a finger into the bay, the occasional white gleam of the buildings, even the fronds of one or two individual palm trees, standing taller than the rest. The only thing he couldn't see was the beach, because at high tide, as it was now, the water covered most of the sand, lapping right up to the trees.

Greg sighed. Butterfly looked good from this angle, which was why they brought guests out here, to this particular section of the reef. The resort's glass-bottomed boat was moored permanently nearby; he'd told Mary he was coming out to clean it up a bit, and he would, too, later on; but first he had other plans.

He looked further along the reef. Another workboat, bigger than his, rode at anchor a few hundred metres away. Greg studied it closely, and decided that he hadn't seen it before. There was nobody aboard, but that wasn't unusual; they were probably down diving along the edge of the reef.

Suddenly the rope stopped running, but Greg paid out a few more metres, leaning over the side to watch the coils snaking down into the clear water. Then he held it fast, like a giant fishing line, and waited. The boat drifted for a while, until it reached the end of its tether, and Greg felt the rope tug at his hand and let go, tug and let go, as the anchor dragged across the sandy bottom. Then he felt a solid, unyielding resistance, and the line angled up out of the water, bowline taut; the anchor had finally taken hold. The change in the motion of the deck under his feet and the hard 'slap, slap' of water against aluminium told Greg that the drifting had stopped, so he took a few deft turns around a cleat to make fast, then moved aft to put on his diving gear.

The boat swung around until it was perfectly positioned, in clear water over a sandy bottom, but only about five metres from the edge of the coral, a dark mass rippling below the surface. In a few minutes he'd be down there; his troubles would be a zillion light years away. Greg normally wasn't the type to brood, but he felt responsible for yesterday's disasters: if he hadn't been careless with the keys, *Elizabeth* would never have been stolen, Jackie wouldn't have been scared out of her wits, and they'd still have ten good canoes. They would never even have *heard* of that kid! He felt that he'd let his father down, and that made him feel pretty bad. As he donned his flippers, he had a further twinge of conscience: Charlie had expressly forbidden him to dive alone. But, Greg argued with himself, he needed a bit of a buzz, and he knew he'd get that down below. Besides, his father would never know. Dismissing further doubt from his mind, he sat on the gunwale, back to the water, checked his mouthpiece, and then tumbled neatly over the side.

He was instantly enveloped in a blur of bubbles, but these quickly cleared, rising like a curtain, and he found himself in another world. He was suspended in crystal space, in water so clear that it didn't seem to be there.

The dark silhouette of his boat was now hanging from a mirrored ceiling, just a few feet above his head, with the thin line of the rope curving down to the anchor, easily visible on the white sandy bottom far below.

Greg looked around and down: on three sides water and sea-floor reached off into the distance until they merged and became a pale, blue-green nothingness; but in the other direction, a forest of coral rose out of the sand, stretching out on either side until it too merged into the void and was lost to view. Troubles already forgotten, completely absorbed in the fantastic variety of colours and shapes of the living reef, Greg finned slowly towards a bommie; a coral outcrop rising almost to the shining surface above. He could identify some of the corals that grew there; the staghorns, with their sturdy branches, the bright red, delicately veined fans swaying to and fro in the current, and the plates, like huge, multi-coloured fungi, securely anchored to the coral rock. There were soft corals, too, with delicate tentacles reaching out into the water in the constant search for food, but Greg gave *all* tentacles a wide berth, no matter how attractive they seemed. He knew from experience that most were capable of inflicting a sting, the effects ranging from a mild tingling to paralysing pain. He kept well clear, too, of the giant clam that he now saw lying half-concealed and gaping among the coral rubble littering the sea-floor: the metre-long shell could easily snap shut, trapping an unwary diver's foot.

But it was the fish that fascinated Greg most. Red, orange, brown, green, purple, brilliant silver, bright electric blue; spotted, striped, camouflaged, flamboyant, elegant, ugly, shy, aggressive, filmy-finned, armed with venomous spines; they were there in their thousands, living on, in, and among the coral. They were breeding, feeding and being fed upon, even in death providing sustenance for another creature which in its turn would reproduce and then die, playing its part, too, in the incredibly complicated, delicately balanced cycle of the reef. As Greg swam closer, glittering swarms of fry, thousands of fish each a few millimetres long, darted around his head like gnats on a summer evening, taking care to keep their distance from their bigger cousins, now beginning to gather, because they knew why the visitor from above was here.

Reaching into a canvas bag that was slung around one shoulder, Greg withdrew a piece of fish flesh and held it out in his fingertips. There was a sudden flurry and it disappeared, snapped up in an instant by a parrot fish, a blur of green and blue. He held out a second piece. Another sudden movement and *that* was gone, too.

Greg finned away, and the fish followed, circling, manoeuvring, jostling, ever-ready to dart in for the next morsel, but they'd had their chance; now it was time for the main event. Greg swam along the coral cliff until he reached a cave that opened, dark and mysterious, under a huge coral rock. He hovered, using easy movements of hands and flippers to maintain position, and reached once more into his bag. He took out a particularly tasty morsel and held it up. This was the moment he had been waiting for, all day.

Suddenly a monstrous shape materialised out of the gloom of the cave mouth. A massive head appeared, then stopped, fins flicking while it examined Greg with its cold, unblinking eyes, the huge gills pulsating slowly as it breathed.

Henry.

The whole family had decided on that name, some years ago: It was either Henry or Henrietta, because they didn't know what sex it was, but Jackie had argued that no *girl* could ever be so *ugly*!

Henry emerged into open water now, and Greg turned with it as it idled past. It didn't pay to take your eyes off a fifty-kilo groper! Not for a second! The huge fish stopped again and slowly drifted around in its own length, eyes on the tasty piece of fish in Greg's extended fingers. Greg felt alone and vulnerable; the cloud of greedy smaller fry had gone now. You couldn't blame them: Henry could swallow a semi-trailer!

Suddenly the groper lunged. Greg let go just in time, and the food was gone, engulfed by the cavernous mouth. The big fish edged backwards, then hovered again, fins still flicking, eye rolling expectantly to focus on the now empty hand, making Greg feel decidedly nervous. Piece of fish or piece of boy; it was probably all the same to Henry! Greg quickly took another morsel out of the canvas bag. *Lunge! Gulp!* Gone, too!

It wasn't long before the canvas bag was empty. Time to go. Keeping a wary eye on Henry, Greg began to edge slowly away from the cave. This was the critical part of the whole operation, because if he was not satisfied, there was nothing to stop the groper biting the hand that had fed him. It wasn't likely; Henry hadn't made a single threatening move in all these years, but with a monster like that, you could never be quite sure.

Suddenly Greg felt a tremendous shock that struck him with the speed and power of a thundering express, forcing him sideways through the water at terrific speed. He felt an excruciating pressure on his head and his ears began to convulse as if they were about to turn inside out. He screamed in agony, spitting out his mouthpiece, which flapped uselessly in front of his face. He swallowed water, coughed, and swallowed more. There was an unrelenting, maddening, buzzing inside his head, his lungs were bursting, and the reef, the water, the fish, the sand, whirled around in front of his eyes, then gradually faded from view to be replaced by a pulsating blackness, tinged with red. He knew he was blacking out, that he must have oxygen, and he fumbled around trying to locate his mouthpiece; but his flailing arms found nothing, and as consciousness receded he became aware of a floating sensation, floating, floating . . . it was quite pleasant, really, because at least the pain was going away, too.

Then, quite unexpectedly, he found himself gulping greedily at fresh, pure air and gazing up at blue sky and white clouds. And there was his boat, still anchored peacefully close by! Summoning all his energy, Greg managed to thrash across the few intervening metres and grab the side. Never had hard aluminium felt so good! He rested for a moment, and then, with a super-human effort, dragged himself aboard, and collapsed in a heap on the deck.

He struggled out of his tank and lay there, panting, gazing up at the sky. He knew he was safe, but he felt most peculiar. His surroundings had taken on a strange, unreal quality, as if in a dream. He could feel the motion of the boat, but there was no slapping of the waves against the hull; the breeze was blowing cool on his shoulders, but it was a silent wind; gulls were wheeling overhead, but he missed their familiar screeching. Suddenly the awful truth sank in: he was stone deaf; he couldn't hear a thing! Overcome by shock and ex-haustion, he closed his eyes, and, lulled by the easy motion of the boat and the welcome warmth of the sun, was asleep at once.

Mary Travers watched as Charlie brought *Elizabeth* in to the Butterfly Island wharf. Sally stepped nimbly across the gap between ship and jetty, and Jackie followed, grinning like a Cheshire cat. 'One extra for dinner, Mary,' she said expansively, pointing with a flourish back into the wheelhouse. Mary gaped. There, behind Charlie, stood the Vietnamese boy! 'His name's Vo Diem,' Jackie said.

Charlie switched off and came to the wheelhouse door. At the sight of Mary's incredulous face he grinned. 'It was your idea,' he said to Jackie. 'You explain.'

But Mary held up her hand. Explanations could wait. Right now there was something more important on her mind. 'Greg missed his science lesson,' she called. 'He hasn't come back from the reef.'

Charlie's face clouded. 'What's he doing out there?'

'He said something about cleaning up the glass-bottomed boat,' she explained, 'but that was three hours ago.'

'He'll turn up,' said Charlie, catching Vo Diem's eye and jerking a thumb towards the wharf.

'There's more,' said Mary, as the boy obeyed. Something in her tone made Charlie feel uneasy.

'There was an explosion,' she said.

Charlie's normally tanned face suddenly grew pale. Without another word he stepped back into the wheelhouse. The engines roared into life again and *Elizabeth* surged away from the wharf in a flurry of foam and diesel fumes as he turned her savagely, heading back towards the open sea.

Greg hated people making a fuss, especially where he was concerned; and he was the centre of attention right now, as he lay back on the couch in the guest lounge, with Mary and Sally buzzing about bringing him tea and blankets and cushions and aspirin and constantly asking him how he felt.

The truth was, he felt a bit shook-up; weak, and wobbly at the knees. He had a terrible headache; the worst he'd ever had in his life. It had woken him up, shortly before Charlie had reached him, but with the pain had come good news: he'd been able to hear the rumble of *Elizabeth's* engines as she came bearing down. His hearing had improved steadily ever since, so he hadn't bothered to mention to anyone that he'd been deafened by the explosion. That would have caused a hell of a fuss, and his Dad would have insisted on a trip over to the doc., for sure.

Charlie came into the room. He'd been on the two-way radio. 'The Marine Studies boys had no one out there today,' he announced. 'They don't know anything about it.'

'Who else would be detonating on the reef?' Mary asked.

Charlie had no idea. He turned to Greg. 'Didn't that boat have any flags up, any signals at all?'

The boy shook his head. 'Nothing, Dad, honest. I just thought they were diving.'

'Fishing more like,' said Charlie angrily. 'But not professionals. Probably ratbags using dynamite to get a quick haul. I'll let Pat know. Nothing else we can do, I suppose.'

Sally reached forward to feel Greg's forehead. 'How do you feel?' she asked for the umpteenth time. 'You don't seem to have a temperature.'

He brushed her hand aside. 'I'm OK, Sally,' he said testily. 'A bit shook-up, that's all.'

'Well, take it easy,' ordered Charlie, then caught Sally's eye. 'Time we had a talk, young lady,' he said, and pointed towards the office. She stood up and left the room without a word. She'd been waiting for this: he was about to give her the big lecture about being a naughty girl and taking things into her own hands. Well, she wasn't just going to stand there and take it, and by the time they'd entered the room Sally had decided to fight fire with fire.

'Suppose I'd made it to Charters Towers, Dad?' she said, taking the initiative almost before he'd finished closing the door. 'Would you have backed me up?'

'That's not the point!' Charlie began, taken off guard. He'd expected to fire the opening shot.

'It's the *only* point that matters to *me*!' insisted Sally. 'Suppose I'd actually managed to book Snowy Rivers for Butterfly? Would you have backed me up?'

Charlie wouldn't be drawn on that. 'What are you

trying to *do* to this place? Turn it into some kind of day-tripper disco?' he asked.

'We would have packed this place out for two weeks!'

'Yes, but with what?' Charlie countered. 'I've seen films of pop festivals. Have you seen how they leave a place?'

Sally was exasperated. 'No one's going to lend you the money you need, Dad. We've got to make it by ourselves.'

'What do you want me to do?' he demanded. 'Dump a few hundred tonnes of concrete on the place? Bulldoze the bush, throw up a funpark?' He was quite agitated now. 'This is the most beautiful island on the Reef, Sally. It's unique. The people I want to attract are the ones who want to share that with me!'

She didn't reply at once, but stood there, watching as he paced around the room. She understood everything he had said, but her father was an idealist, through and through; he was talking about the Reef as it had been when he was a boy; and that was a long time ago.

Eventually she spoke. 'I'm on your side, Dad,' she said, sadly. 'But you won't let me help you. You won't let anyone help you.' Close to tears, she swept from the room.

In the lounge Greg was growing restless and increasingly uncomfortable as he lay on the couch, attracting curious stares from passing guests. He wasn't an *invalid*, for crying out loud! Finally he could stand it no longer and, throwing off the blanket, he tottered towards Reception on his decidedly unsteady legs. His timing couldn't have been worse, because just as he was passing the counter, Mary came into the room.

'Don't you think you'd be better if you rested?' she asked kindly. Greg shook his head, trying hard to keep his temper under control. If one more person was kind and understanding he was going to blow a valve!

'There's something I want to do,' he said.

'You've got to be *kidding*!' she exclaimed, and bustled towards him, ready to escort him back to the couch.

'I'm *all right*, Mary!' His tone stopped her in her tracks. She shrugged, waiting to see what he would do.

'Why did Dad bring that kid back here?' he asked.

'So they wouldn't send him to the Remand Centre.'

He raised his eyebrows, 'That was a dumb idea.'

'Now *you* tell *me* something,' she asked, following up. 'Do you know anyone *else* around here who would have done that?' He shook his head, and Mary went on, her expression softening as she spoke: 'That's one of the things that makes your Dad special, Greg.'

He left her then, and made his way to the workshop, where he collected a small spanner, a padlock, and a length of chain. He went down to the beach, where the Resort's aluminium dinghies were drawn up on the sand. In a few minutes he had linked them all together with the chain. He then passed the chain around one of the wooden jetty piles, and secured the padlock with a satisfying 'click!'. 'Let the kid try to pinch a boat *now*! Then he turned his attention to the small outboard motors, using the spanner to remove the petrol leads.

Charlie was in the workshop when he returned. 'Why aren't you inside?' he asked.

'I've chained and padlocked the boats, Dad,' Greg announced, 'And I'm locking *these* in the office.' Charlie's eyes went to the fuel leads, hooked over his arm. It was obvious that Greg was taking the Vietnamese boy's presence on the island very seriously: perhaps *too* seriously.

'Well, unless he can grow wings, Vo Diem's here for the duration, then,' he grinned, trying to lighten the mood. Greg's expression remained hard and disapproving. 'Trying to do the right thing hardly ever makes life easier, son,' Charlie said gently, but Greg was in no mood for philosophising.

'Suppose he smashes something else?' he asked bluntly.

By way of reply, Charlie rummaged in a box of odds and ends and selected a sturdy bolt. 'He'll be locked in at night,' he said, holding it up. 'Properly, this time. And you were right ahead of me there,' he went on, pointing to the petrol leads.

For the first time since he'd entered the workshop, Greg grinned.

Vo Diem sat on the bed in the spare room, from which he had so recently escaped, and looked around. Nothing had changed. The windows were still shuttered, and he was about to go over to test the lock on the door when it opened, and Jackie came into the room carrying a tray which she set down on the bed beside him. 'Stew and potatoes,' she said, nodding at the food.

He stared at it, taking care to give no indication that he had understood. Jackie crossed the room to a chair that faced the bed, sat down, and waited. Diem knew what she wanted him to do, and he was hungry, but he wasn't going to give in right away. Avoiding her gaze, he looked around the room, then at the food, then at the patient, unrelenting girl. Finally, honour satisfied, he picked up the plate.

'Watch out! It's hot!' Jackie spoke before the spoon touched his lips, trying to trick him into a reaction, but he was too clever for that, letting the hot food burn his mouth before he allowed his expression to change. He put the plate down to allow the food to cool, then looked back at Jackie, who kept her eyes fixed resolutely on his, capitalising on his uncertainty, making him wonder what she was going to do next. Then she stood up and moved across the room, turning as she reached the door: 'We needn't have bothered bringing you back here, you know,' she said. 'Your uncle's on his way right now.' The words were delivered as an afterthought, and they had the desired effect. Jackie saw a barely detectable reaction from the boy; just a tightening of his face muscles; but it was enough. 'You do understand English, don't you?' she said, accusingly.

Vo Diem didn't reply, keeping his bluff going until the bitter end. 'Dad was right when he said we couldn't trust you,' said Jackie, one hand on the door knob. She turned to go.

'Why did you bring me here?'

At the sound of his voice, she stopped, jubilant; she'd had a win, however small! She turned back to face him, taking care not to let her elation show. 'Because we felt sorry for you, despite what you did to our canoes,' she said.

'When will my uncle get here?' he asked, ignoring her accusation. His English, although heavily accented, was quite good.

'I don't know,' shrugged Jackie. 'I just said that to see what you'd do.'

Charlie was not at all pleased to hear of the deception, and summoned Vo Diem to the family-room. He was having serious doubts about his decision to bring the Vietnamese boy back to Butterfly, and he was letting his feelings show.

'While you're here, you'll do as you're told!' he barked, pacing up and down like a sergeant-major. 'And you'll help Jackie and Greg with the work that has to be done. Right?'

Diem nodded; his instinct for self-preservation told him that it would be extreme folly to do otherwise.

'Behave yourself, and you'll have the run of the place,' Charlie went on. 'Do the wrong thing, and you'll stay in that room under lock and key. Understood?'

The boy nodded again, but that wasn't good enough. Charlie waited for more.

'Understood,' said Diem, catching on fast.

'Right,' nodded Charlie, satisfied. 'Show him the ropes, Jackie.'

'Come on,' she said, and led him from the room.

When they had gone, Mary broke the tension. 'I don't think anyone's given that kid a break in a long time,' she said with a smile.

Charlie scratched his head. 'Well, I hope *I* haven't made a big mistake,' he replied.

It was feeding time for Jackie's lorikeets, and she stood, plate of bread and honey in hand, the brightly-coloured red and green birds swarming over her shoulders and arms, and fluttering around her head. Mindful of Charlie's orders, Vo Diem dutifully held a plate too, but there were no birds anywhere near him, because whenever one approached, he would shoo it away with an uneasy hand. Jackie was amused: he could stow away on a plane and steal a boat, but here he was, frightened by a few lorikeets! 'We have to feed the birds every day,' she explained, 'so they'll expect it during the tourist season.' He shrugged. As long as they stayed well clear, he couldn't care less.

There was a short pause, punctuated by the harsh screeching of the feeding birds. Finally, Jackie spoke. 'Why did you smash the canoes, Vo?' she asked disarmingly, taking care to keep her eyes off his face.

'My name is Diem.' He replied at once, correcting her; then added, 'I did not do it.'

She threw him a shrewd, questioning glance. Was this another lie? 'Who did, then?' she asked.

He shook his head. 'When I got to the beach that morning, the canoes were already smashed.'

'Why didn't you tell Dad? Or Sergeant Connolly?' asked Jackie.

He smiled bitterly. 'They wouldn't believe me.'

She nodded. He was right.

Later in the morning she took him into the family's Reef Museum and watched as he wandered slowly around the room, examining the specimens with great interest. The carapace of a monstrous green turtle dominated one wall, with a two-metre long 'saw' from a sawfish mounted underneath, alongside that were the gaping jaws of a tiger shark. Jackie smiled to herself as he reached up, fascinated, and ran his finger over the razor-sharp, multi-layered teeth.

She opened a varnished cabinet, and Diem came and stood beside her, eager to see what lay inside. The drawer was full of shells, all carefully graduated and labelled, the result of years of informed fossicking up and down the Great Barrier Reef. There was a range of beautiful, highly-polished cowries, trochus shells, spider shells, rare kookaburra shells, looking for all the world like miniatures of the much-loved Australian bird, and the beautiful but deadly cone shells that could kill almost instantly with their paralysing sting.

'I look after this room,' said Jackie proudly, closing the drawer, and as if to prove it she opened a cupboard and took out a dusting cloth with a flourish. 'You can sweep the floor, but be careful,' she ordered, handing him a broom. He obeyed without question, working industriously, as if in deference to the treasures ranged around the room. 'This was my mother's collection,' she continued, carefully wiping a giant bailer shell with the cloth.

'She's a good cook,' said Diem.

'No, that's Mary,' corrected Jackie, shaking her head. This kid was getting all confused. 'Mary's our *housekeeper*. My mother died seven years ago.'

Her words had more impact than she knew. Vo Diem paused and leant on his broom, looking at Jackie with a new understanding, mingled with hope. This girl had suffered the loss of a parent; perhaps she would soon begin to comprehend how *he* felt.

They moved down to the beach then, and Jackie was putting him to work hosing out the boats when Sally came up to announce that they were both wanted at the house in half an hour. 'How are you feeling?' she asked him, with genuine concern, but he ignored her, playing the jet of water noisily on the metal hulls.

Sally poked a face. 'I'm very *well*, thanks, Sally!' she exclaimed sarcastically, answering her own question. 'Nice of you to *ask*!' She turned to Jackie. 'Half an hour,' she said, and walked off in a huff.

Jackie turned off the tap. 'Why didn't you say something?' she blazed. 'Don't you know she probably saved your life?' The Vietnamese boy began to coil the hose without a word. Jackie was thoroughly annoyed now. 'What's wrong with you? You can't hate *everybody!*' she said, then stormed off, expecting him to follow, but Diem delayed for a few seconds, taking advantage of the time to examine Greg's chain, lifting it thoughtfully with his foot before trudging off after her across the sand.

Half an hour later Jackie was still letting off steam. 'He's an ungrateful rat!' she fumed, furiously towelling her hair after a swim in the Resort pool.

'It's no big deal, Jackie,' said Sally, who was standing with her beside the pool.

'The least he could have done was say thank you,' Jackie went on, threatening to decapitate herself with the towel.

'The boy isn't playing your game, eh Jackie?' said Mary, as she placed a bowl of salad on the poolside table. The Wilsons were going to eat outdoors this evening, as they often did, all year round, except in the wet. 'He's not grateful enough, eh?'

Greg, still in the pool, interjected. 'Yeah; grateful enough to smash our canoes!'

'We don't know that for certain, Greg,' responded

Jackie. His eyebrows shot up; why should she be on the defensive?

'You said he denied doing it,' said Mary.

'Probably just another lie,' grunted Greg, floating on his back. He submerged briefly, took a mouthful, and squirted a jet of water high into the air.

Mary smiled sadly. 'More than likely he's been lying and stealing since he was old enough to walk, just to survive,' she said.

'But surely he can see we want to *help* him!' exclaimed Jackie, confused.

'We keep locking him up,' replied Mary. 'You can hardly expect him to say "thank you".'

Jackie had no asnwer to that. Baffled, she looked towards the mainland where the sun was about to disappear behind the mountains, setting the sky on fire, and reflecting its golden brilliance across the still waters of the lagoon.

There was no such magnificent view for Vo Diem, because he was sitting on the bed in the spare room, watching the bolt being attached firmly to the door. Charlie worked in silence, but when the job was finished, he stood up and turned to face him. 'Did Jackie show you what had to be done?' he asked.

'I did the work,' the boy replied, defensively.

'Oh, I know that,' Charlie said. 'Everybody has to work here. That's how this family survives.' He was trying to find some kind of common ground, so that they could begin to communicate.

'I did the work,' Vo Diem repeated.

'That's not the point!' exclaimed Charlie, annoyed. 'That's not why I let my daughter talk me into bringing you here!' The kid was simply refusing, point blank, to play ball.

'Why *did* you bring me here?' asked Diem.

'Because I felt sorry for you!' replied Charlie. 'The

least you could do is show half an ounce of gratitude!'

'For what?' retorted the boy angrily.

'You'd be in the Remand Centre by now, if I hadn't taken responsibility for you!'

Diem jumped to his feet. 'You took me from a place with locks on the door!' he cried out, agitatedly. 'You bring me here, and you put *more* locks on the door! Why should I be grateful to be locked up?'

Charlie paused for a moment before he replied; at least he was getting some sort of emotional response; maybe at long last he was beginning to get through. 'Now, hold on a minute, son,' he said, firmly but kindly. 'No one here wants to take precautions like this. We're not your enemies. We want to help you. Now I know you've had a rough time where you come from. . . .'

The boy cut him short. 'You don't know about where I come from! You're *rich*!' It was an accusation, not a statement of fact. 'I don't *want* your lousy help!' He turned away. Subject ended. Without another word, Charlie left the room, closing the door behind him, and Diem heard the sound of the bolt sliding home. His jaw hardened with determination; this man Wilson might have bolted the door, but he'd overlooked the fact that the hinges were on the inside. Reaching into his shirt, he produced a screwdriver that he'd managed to 'acquire' while dragging around after Jackie during the afternoon.

It was almost dark when Jackie came upon Greg in the bush, as he was stringing lengths of rope through the undergrowth and stretching them across the sandy path that led to the beach. 'Promise you won't tell Dad,' he said, almost guiltily.

'Tell him what?' she said. How could she? She didn't even know what he was up to . . . yet!

'Are you going to promise, or not?' he insisted.

'All right, I promise,' she said impatiently.

'Well,' said Greg, rubbing his hands together enthusiastically, 'it's a kind of alarm.'

'An alarm against what?'

'That kid said he didn't wreck the canoes,' he answered.

Jackie sighed. 'I thought you didn't believe him.'

'I don't,' affirmed Greg. 'But if it *is* someone else, I want to be ready for them.' He held up one of the ropes and in the half light she could make out the shapes of a dozen or so tin cans, attached at regular intervals along its length.

'You wouldn't hear those rattle from the house,' she said, sceptically.

He'd thought of that. 'I'll be keeping watch from out here,' he said.

'You'll be in trouble if Dad finds out.'

He glared at her. 'You *promised*!' he said.

'I know,' she replied testily: it had been a warning, not a threat.

'Give us a hand then.' She'd been waiting for the invitation, and together they began to stretch another ropeful of cans.

There was no moon that night, and it was very still and very quiet, the only sound being a gentle 'shoosh' now and then as a wave kissed the sand. Charlie sat alone in the dark, on an upturned hull on the beach, feeling apprehensive and depressed. Earlier in the evening he'd received a call from David Lee, the manager of Reef Royale, a big tourist resort about twenty kilometres away to the south. He was just sitting down to dinner when the call came through: an inconvenient time; typical of Lee, who wanted a business meeting as soon as possible. Charlie had tried to put him off: there was nothing that he wanted to discuss with David Lee, particularly in the light of recent events on Butterfly Island, but vultures always knew when to strike, and

Lee must have got wind of their misfortunes somehow. He was accustomed to getting his own way, and in the end Charlie had agreed to go across to Reef Royale in the morning, just to get rid of him. He'd regretted it ever since.

Another wave slid up on to the sand, sprinkling it with hundreds of little pinpoints of phosphorescent light. Charlie leant back on his elbows and began to unwind. There was nothing to be gained by brooding: he'd find out what Lee wanted tomorrow, and that was probably soon enough. He surrendered his troubled soul to the tranquillity of the night, and looked up into the sky, searching among the blazing stars for the familiar formation of the Southern Cross. A meteorite slashed a brief, fiery path overhead, and as the embers of its passage faded into the night, his eye was attracted by another, steadier movement; a satellite, on its silent, lonely journey around the world.

The peace was suddenly marred by a discordant, metallic clanking, followed by the sound of Greg's voice. Charlie heard him yell, 'Hey!' and then, after a short pause, 'Hey! You!' He jumped up. What in heaven's name was Greg *doing*, out of bed at this time of night?

Somewhere near the source of the sound a torch came on and waved around erratically. Charlie sprinted down the beach towards the light, but before he could reach it he felt something wrap itself around his foot, and he fell flat on his face in the darkness to the accompaniment of clanking cans. He came up cursing and spitting sand to see Greg on the ground nearby, holding the torch with one hand and his head with the other, trying at the same time to stand up.

'What the blazes is going on?' Charlie yelled.

'Someone hit me!' gasped Greg, dazed.

'Someone?' cried Charlie, helping him up. 'Which way?' Greg pointed a groggy finger in the general direction of the jetty. Charlie took the torch and switched it off. 'Come on!' he whispered.

They reached the jetty and paused, straining eyes and ears, but the seaward end was lost in the blackness. Charlie moved forward, one step at a time, Greg keeping very close, until the shape of the *Elizabeth* materialised out of the gloom. Carefully, quietly, Charlie stepped aboard, then moved to the wheelhouse door. He threw it open and snapped on the torch, but the sudden beam of light revealed no surprises; crouching on the deck was Vo Diem.

'It's all my fault,' said Jackie, when their prisoner was once more under lock and key. 'I'm sorry, Greg. You could have been hurt.'

'What do you mean "*could have*"?' he said indignantly, rubbing his head.

'I'm sorry,' she said again.

'Yeah,' Greg replied, uncomfortably. Jackie looked at him sharply. She could read her brother like a book, and something was bothering him; something more than a bump on the head; maybe the explosion that afternoon.

'What's the matter, Greg?' she asked.

'Well,' he began, scratching his chin doubtfully. 'I can't be sure, but . . .'

'About what?' she interrupted.

'Well,' he continued thoughtfully, 'that kid isn't very big.'

'So?'

Greg met her eyes. 'I got hit *hard*, that's all. I can't be sure, but I think whoever knocked me down out there was a damned sight bigger than Vo Diem!'

FIVE

David Lee's resort was located on Royal Island, hence its name: Reef Royale; and Charlie hated the place. In the space of two years the island had been transformed. First, bulldozers had moved in, knocking down whole stands of native trees and ripping the guts out of the hillsides, leaving ugly scars that were visible for miles out to sea; then a conglomeration of ultra-modern, hard-edged units, huge pools, tennis courts and other 'facilities' had grown up almost overnight. The buildings themselves were obviously not cheap, but they seemed to be a hotch-potch combination of Polynesian, Melanesian, and Malaysian architectural styles, with a bit of Mediterranean thrown in. Reef Royale was big, brash and, in Charlie's eyes, far from beautiful; it just didn't belong on the Barrier Reef. By comparison Butterfly was Queensland Chaotic, small, old, and, he had to admit, a bit run-down, but it was picturesque, genuine, and warm and friendly, for all that.

He was sitting in the ante-room of Lee's office, reflecting on these matters when the secretary, a beautifully-groomed girl with a posh Melbourne accent, interrupted his train of thought to tell him that he could go in.

The man himself came to the door to meet him. David Lee was of average height, slightly-built, tanned, and dressed in an ornately-printed open-necked shirt and immaculately tailored casual slacks. He looked more like a used-car salesman than a man of influence and power, but appearances were always deceptive where Lee was concerned.

'Good to see you, Charlie,' he beamed. 'It doesn't happen often enough.'

'No,' said Charlie, shaking the proffered hand without enthusiasm. 'Only when you want something. First time you've bothered with the red carpet treatment, though.' Lee had sent a V.I.P. helicopter across to Butterfly to pick him up.

The businessman shrugged, smiled again, and indicated a chair. He retreated behind his desk. 'Can I offer you a drink?' he asked.

'No thanks. You can get to the point.'

Lee nodded. 'I appreciate that, Charlie. No need to beat about the bush.'

Charlie leaned forward in his seat. 'If it's that day-tripper deal again, forget it. I'm not having your guests charging about all over my island.'

But David Lee waved his remarks aside. 'It's bigger than that,' he said, coming around to the front of his desk again. 'It's a deal to safeguard your family's future.' He paused, standing over Charlie, then leant down for dramatic effect. 'You let me have Butterfly Island, and I'll pay you one million dollars.'

Charlie didn't reply at once. He couldn't. Lee's offer had taken him completely by surprise. For several long seconds he just sat, stunned, his mind racing to grasp the full import of the words.

The response, when it *did* come, was typical. Charlie grinned: an amused, crooked grin, zig-zagging across his sun-tanned face.

Lee smiled politely. 'I'm glad you've got a sense of humour, Charlie,' he said calmly. 'Perhaps you'd be good enough to explain the joke to *me*.'

Charlie nodded. He had the offer in its proper perspective now. 'Even if I considered selling the island, one million dollars is a *long way* short of the mark,' he said. It was a simple statement, because in money matters, Charlie Wilson was a simple man. He meant what he said, nothing more, nothing less; but David Lee interpreted his words as a clumsy attempt to hold out for more money, because in his world, every person had a price, anything and everything could be bought. It was just a matter of bargaining, bluffing, threatening, trading off.

'It's a question of perspective, isn't it?' he asked. 'You're looking at your home, one of the most beautiful islands on the Great Barrier Reef.' Then his voice hardened: 'I'm looking at a piece of real estate, mortgaged up to the hilt, totally unable to pay its way.'

Charlie's grin faded. 'It's still no deal,' he said.

'I'm being completely open with you,' went on Lee earnestly. 'I've seen your plans to develop Butterfly along completely environmental lines. Brilliant.'

'Spare me the compliments,' returned Charlie. Flattery embarrassed him at the best of times; coming from Lee it went over like a lead balloon.

'But no one will lend you that amount of money,' pressed Lee. 'Sell the island to me, and I'll make Butterfly the paradise you want it to be.'

Charlie stood up.

'Think about it,' Lee urged, with just a hint of urgency. 'In a couple of months, you may not have any choice.' It was an old salesman's trick; the hurry-up, but Charlie wasn't having any.

He paused at the door. '*No one's* getting their hands on my island, Mr Lee,' he said matter-of-factly. 'Certainly not *you*.' He turned and left, nodding briefly to the secretary as he passed her desk. White-faced, fists clenched in frustration, David Lee could do nothing but watch him go.

Sally, Greg and Jackie were waiting on the beach when the helicopter returned. It came in low, the downwash from its rotors churning the tops of the coconut palms into an uneasy dance. It hovered noisily for a moment, forcing them to cover their faces against the stinging sand, and then it touched, one skid after the other on the sloping beach. The door opened and Charlie stepped down and began to sprint towards them, head down, but he hadn't gone more than a dozen paces before the chopper lifted off again. They all watched the machine turn in its own length and clatter noisily out over the bay.

'What did Mr Lee want, Dad?' It was Jackie who asked the question, but one glance at their faces told Charlie that they were *all* burning to know. Greg made no secret of his curiosity; he was almost panting, like a puppy waiting for a bone, while Sally was trying to appear uninterested, and failing miserably. However, Charlie wasn't sure if he was ready to tell them.

'Same old boring business,' he said, and began to walk away, smiling at the small crowd of curious guests who had been attracted by the helicopter's noise. Despite his confident manner during the interview with David Lee, he was feeling anything but secure. Some of Lee's remarks about mortgages and the resort not paying its way had been uncomfortably close to the truth.

'Did you tell him to jump in the lake?' asked Greg eagerly, when they finally reached the privacy of the office.

'Sure,' said his father, hating himself as he spoke. He wasn't in the habit of withholding things from his kids.

'You don't look as though you told him to jump in the lake.' It was Mary's voice. Charlie looked up sharply to see her standing in the door, regarding him shrewdly.

'Why don't you go and bake a cake, or something?' he growled, feeling worse; she could read him like a book.

Mary ignored his remark. 'Pat Connolly phoned,' she said. 'Vo Diem's uncle flew in this morning. They're coming over here to collect him now.'

'Good,' sighed Charlie wearily, 'that's one problem off our hands.' With that he left the office.

He made his way to the Resort Museum, and stood in the centre of the room, allowing the atmosphere to sink in. The museum was Charlie's sanctuary; whenever he felt depressed or lonely, which was more often that the kids knew, he came here, and invariably, before long, he felt his spirits lift. The room was full of memories; recollections of moments shared with someone very special; reminiscences of a time that now seemed so very long ago. He stood gazing up at the turtle shell, and allowed his mind to wander back to the afternoon when he and Elizabeth had found its occupant dead on the beach. He could even remember the smell! Smiling to himself, he ran his finger over a giant clam shell that was leaning against the wall. He'd almost stepped into it when they were diving in the lagoon. It had been a devil of a job prising it off the bottom, but Elizabeth was a real stand-over merchant where good specimens were concerned. He opened one of the drawers and cast an expert eye over the shells. He'd been with her when she'd collected most of those, too; the majority quite close to the island. Charlie sighed: you had to go a lot further afield to find shells of that size and quality these days.

He was feeling better now; more relaxed; the magic of the museum was working. Charlie sighed again. He didn't believe in the supernatural, or anything like that, but somehow, whenever he was here, he felt that Elizabeth was very close.

He didn't see Sally at the door, but she was watching him. There was a lot she wanted to discuss, yet as soon as she saw his face she knew that this was not the time. She turned and silently walked away, leaving her father to meditate, undisturbed.

Vo Diem sat on his bed, feeling decidedly shaky and

insecure. It had been a traumatic day so far, even though he hadn't been outside the spare room. The noise of Lee's helicopter in the early morning had thrown him into a blind panic, because he'd heard that terrifying sound before, in Vietnam, as the gunships swept in low over the trees like giant, deadly dragon-flies, raking his village with machine-gun fire.

He had cowered under the bed, just as he'd done as his home was destroyed around him, but this time the hail of bullets never came; there were no screams, no smoke, no flames; instead the frightful chopping sound had quickly abated as the machine flew away. And then, an hour or so later it had returned, sending him under the bed again, rigid with fear; but again the bullets didn't come, and the helicopter had once more flown away, leaving him sweating and breathless, almost in shock.

He heard the bolt sliding back, but didn't bother to look up to see who was opening the door.

'You've got visitors, son.' It was Charlie.

Visitors? Here?

Diem sat up apprehensively as an attractive Viet-namese woman in her mid-twenties came into the room. 'I am Michelle Kim,' she said, speaking in Vietnamese, in a friendly but businesslike tone. 'I am a liaison officer. Your uncle has come for you.'

Diem sat bolt upright. Uncle Luong!

He watched sullenly as a slightly-built, tight-lipped Vietnamese man of about Charlie's age came and stood beside the bed. 'I will speak with my nephew alone,' he said coldly.

Charlie got the message, even though he couldn't understand the words. 'I'll leave you to it then,' he said, turning towards the door. Diem found himself des-perately wishing that Charlie would stay, but he kept silent.

'He seems very frightened,' said Michelle, looking

concernedly at Vo Diem as Charlie left the room.

'He should be very *ashamed*,' replied Luong. He nodded towards the open door. The message was clear: she was expected to leave, too, but Michelle hesitated, reluctant to go. Luong glared at her. 'I wish to speak to him *alone!*' His voice had a high-pitched, unpleasant tone. She shrugged, and with a final concerned glance at Vo Diem, left the room.

Luong stood over the bed. 'You have brought disgrace to the family!' he hissed. 'You will return to Brisbane with me, and stay there!'

Diem remained silent, but his defiant expression spoke volumes. No way.

'You will do as I say!' insisted Luong.

'I will run away again, until I find my mother and father!' retorted the boy.

'You must accept the truth, boy, as I have,' snapped Luong. 'Your parents are dead!'

'They're *not* dead!' shouted Diem, jumping up. 'I don't care what you say! They're *not dead*!'

Luong's temples were pulsing with rage. 'You shame me!' he cried. 'You shame the memory of your parents! Your behaviour has caused me to lose face in the eyes of our people, and the officials of this country!' Alarmed, Diem moved away, but his uncle followed him. 'You ungrateful brat! I took you in when you were alone with nowhere to go!' Luong raised his arm in fury, about to strike.

'Mr *Luong!*' Michelle Kim stood at the door.

'This is a family matter,' snapped Luong, but she stood her ground, staring coolly at him until he lowered his arm.

Vo Diem saw his chance, and seized it. He made a rush for the door, pushing roughly past Michelle.

'Hey!' Ignoring her protests he scampered down the corridor, followed by his uncle's angry yells. He came to another door, opened it, and ducked inside. Jackie's room. No shutters on this window! He flung it open, dived, and suddenly he was free!

In the family-room, Mary, Charlie, and Pat Connolly were enjoying a cup of tea when there was a commotion outside, and they looked up to see a distressed Michelle Kim standing at the door. 'Sergeant!' she blurted out, 'Diem has run away!'

'Oh, no!' Charlie froze, cup to lip, but the Sergeant was already on his feet.

'Come on!' he ordered, elbowing Luong out of the way. Charlie followed him outside, and together they made a rapid search around the buildings, but there was no sign of Diem.

Greg came racing up. 'Get down to the jetty, son!' said Charlie. 'Vo Diem's got away.'

'What, *again*?' asked Greg, incredulously.

'Get moving!' roared his father. 'Yell out if you spot him!' As the boy obeyed, Charlie turned to Connolly. 'I hope you've got your boat keys with you,' he said.

Jackie walked alone along the beach, dragging a stick disconsolately through the fine sand. She felt terrible. She didn't know exactly why, but it was something to do with Vo Diem. She was all mixed up. One part of her said that she should be feeling glad that he was going; that it was a good thing that his uncle was coming to take him away, because he'd been nothing but trouble ever since he'd entered their lives. Yet another part of her felt sorry for him because it was quite obvious that he'd been through a lot before coming to Australia. She also admired his guts and his determination and felt that she'd like to help him if she could, but then that made her feel disloyal to her father, she felt guilty about that and then the whole cycle began again. Glad, sorry, disloyal, guilty! What a mess!

Jackie stopped walking and took her feelings out on the stick, flinging it high and hard, watching it turn slowly end-over-end before splashing into the sea. She looked back along the beach, and was surprised to find how far she'd come; the Resort was out of sight around the point. It was time to be heading back.

At this part of the island the shore was rocky, with a narrow beach, the bush coming down almost to the water's edge, and she hadn't gone far, picking her way among the stones, when there was a disturbance and a familiar figure burst out of the undergrowth and fell headlong on to the sand.

'Don't tell them you saw me,' blurted Vo Diem urgently, scrambling to his feet.

'What are *you* doing?' asked Jackie, amazed; he should have left the island *hours* ago.

'Just don't tell them,' he repeated, avoiding the question.

'You should be with your uncle,' she said.

'He would lock me up,' the boy replied warily, and as he backed away she saw that old, hunted look in his eyes. Suddenly he turned and began to run.

'Diem! Wait!' Jackie called. He stopped, and turned. For a split second she paused. She had an idea. It was crazy, but it might just work! 'I know a place where they'll never find you.'

As soon as the words came out she felt better, as if a great weight had suddenly lifted from her mind. Vo Diem hesitated, unsure. 'The island's too small,' she insisted. 'They're sure to catch you out here.' For a moment Jackie thought that he wasn't going to trust her, because he ran up the beach to the edge of the bush. But then he stopped, broke off a tree branch, and ran back, taking great care to step in the footprints that he had already made in the sand.

'Where?' he asked urgently, with a furtive glance back in the direction of the Resort.

'This way,' she said, and waded into the water. Diem waited, puzzled, but didn't move.

'Come *on*!' called Jackie impatiently, already up to her waist. He followed, walking backwards into the sea, sweeping the branch in a fanlike motion as he went, completely obliterating their footprints. She waited until he stood beside her, then, without another word, suddenly dived. Finding himself alone, Diem took a deep breath and eased himself under cautiously, too.

The water was very clear. A few metres ahead he could see where the sea-bed dropped away abruptly over an almost-vertical cliff, and when Jackie swam over the edge he followed, placing his fate entirely in her hands. He kept close behind her as she went down, down, then turned back towards the shore and squeezed through a narrow opening under an overhanging shelf of rock. Diem found himself swimming upwards through a dark passageway, following the flashes of her fluttering feet.

Suddenly he surfaced, and found himself treading water and gulping air while his eyes adjusted to the gloom. They were in a small, dark cave, evidently running back under the rocky shore. He could make out Jackie's shadowy form, sitting on a ledge. She motioned to him and he swam over, hauled himself out of the water, and sat beside her. And then he became aware that the walls and roof of the chamber were pulsating with an eerie green glow. He reached out and touched the rock, then hastily withdrew his hand. The tips of his fingers had begun to glow, too.

'Phosphorescence,' hissed Jackie, close to his ear, but he didn't understand. 'It gives off light. It won't hurt,' she elaborated, rubbing the wall and holding out her finger to show him. Reassured, he tried it again for himself.

'How long can we stay down here?' Vo Diem asked, running his finger over the damp rock. In the confined space, his voice sounded very loud.

'Shh!' whispered Jackie. She held a glowing finger to

her lips, then pointed upwards. 'There's a couple of air passages. Sound carries.' He got the message at once. There was little point in advertising their presence to anyone who happened to be standing above: they'd be hot on his trail by now.

'Greg and I used to come down here all the time,' whispered Jackie.

Diem looked at her in alarm. 'Then he will come and look!' he hissed.

She smiled. She knew Greg. 'I doubt it. You'll be all right for a while,' she said. There was silence for a moment, as Diem contemplated the watery floor, rising and falling in time with the ocean's swell.

'Jackie. That's a boy's name,' he said.

'It's short for Jacqueline,' Jackie laughed. 'Anyway, your name's funny, too!'

He looked at her in surprise. What could possibly be funny about a name like Vo Diem? 'Vo Diem,' Jackie went on, emphasising both words. 'We should call you Vo.'

He shook his head. 'Vo is my *family* name. *My* name is Diem.'

She looked straight at him. 'Diem, why are you running away?'

He didn't answer at once, but returned her gaze, probing her searching eyes with his own. He could see no danger there; only honesty, and an earnest desire to help. This girl, Jackie, deserved to *know*.

He reached into his shirt and pulled out a folded plastic bag, which he carefully unwrapped to reveal a battered black-and-white photograph. Jackie bent over to look. It was hard to make out the details in the poor light, but she could identify Diem, and a man and a woman, both Vietnamese. His parents? One look at his face told her that she didn't need to ask. 'They're not dead,' said the boy. 'I have to find them.'

'Where are they?' asked Jackie.

94

'Their boat was lost near Indonesia. I will find them there.'

'Indonesia?' Jackie was astounded. 'That's thousands of kilometres away!'

'I will get there,' said Diem determinedly.

'It's impossible!' Jackie scoffed.

'What would *you* do?' he asked, quietly.

She didn't answer, but deep down inside she knew that if she were in Diem's shoes she'd be on *her* way back to Indonesia, too.

The search had widened from the immediate vicinity of the Resort now, and the searchers had spread out, each combing a particular section of the thick scrub. Sergeant Connolly was working his way along a narrow, overgrown track, obviously little-used. Butterfly was a hilly island, the ground rising quite sharply not far inland, and the going was rough. To make matters worse, it was a hot, humid day, with no cooling breeze in the bush once you moved away from the sea, so his shirt was saturated with perspiration, clinging to his big frame like a wet dish-rag.

Suddenly Connolly thought he heard a noise. He stopped to listen, glad of the opportunity to catch his breath. Yes, there it was: the swish of bushes and the crackling of twigs. Someone was moving through the undergrowth just ahead. The policeman squeezed his bulk behind a tree and waited. The noise came closer. Connolly smiled: the kid didn't know how to move through the bush; he was making as much noise as a Sherman Tank! But then, from what he'd read, they didn't have much bush left in Vietnam; the Yanks had sprayed chemicals on the trees. The boy was close now; Connolly could distinguish individual footsteps. The policeman readied himself, and when he judged the moment right, lunged through the bushes, and grabbed.

'Crikey!' yelled Greg.

'Oh! Sorry son!' said the sergeant, instantly letting go. 'I thought you were Vo Diem.'

'Wow!' Greg was rubbing his shoulder where the policeman's huge hand had taken hold. 'Is that what it's like to be arrested?'

'Now you know,' Connolly chuckled, then pointed ahead, to where the trail forked at a big tree. 'You take the left-hand track,' he said.

'Right, Sergeant,' agreed Greg. He was on the move before the policeman had finished speaking, and disappeared almost at once, but as Connolly ambled up to the fork and turned right he could still hear him, crashing his way through the undergrowth like a rampaging bulldozer.

The track the Sergeant had chosen meandered towards the sea, and he emerged on to a rocky shore, bursting out on to the narrow beach almost before he knew it, because the bush grew down very close to the water's edge. He paused for a moment, enjoying the cool sea breeze, and looked back towards the Resort. The buildings were out of sight around the point, but in the distance he could see Charlie's diminutive figure making his way towards him along the beach.

And then he spotted the tracks.

A set of footprints came out of the bush, went down to the water's edge, and then came back again. Connolly waved urgently to Charlie, watched as the distant figure began to run, and then trudged over to give the footprints a more detailed inspection.

The tracks were Diem's size, but there was something odd about them. In twenty-five years in the North, Pat Connolly had picked up a few pointers from the black trackers, who could almost tell you the colour of a fugitive's eyes by studying a single bent blade of grass. Connolly wasn't in that league, but he could read the basic signs, and there was something here that didn't quite ring true. He followed the trail, squatting down to examine each imprint, then moved on, studying the marks one by one.

The tracks going down to the water were standard; the shape of a foot with toe and heel marks pressing firmly and smoothly to make a clear-cut indentation in the sand, but the marks leading up to the bush were different; the indentations were deeper, with the edges broken in places, as if a second impression had been made soon after the first. Connolly's sharp eye detected something else, too; a faint disturbance in the surface of the sand; just the slightest change in texture over a strip about three feet wide, running from the bush down to the water.

He stood up and thought for a while, and when Charlie arrived he had it all worked out. 'He came down to the beach, retraced his tracks so we'd think he'd gone back into the bush, and covered his footprints with this,' he announced, brandishing the branch that he'd found lying on the sand.

'Cunning little fox, I'll say that for him,' declared Charlie, out of breath.

'He's got to come out of the water somewhere,' said the Sergeant. 'I think we'd better split up.' Charlie nodded agreement and both men turned and headed off in opposite directions along the beach, eyes down, looking for more tell-tale signs on the sand.

In the cave, Jackie was growing restless. She didn't have her watch, but she was certain she'd been away from the Resort for hours. 'I'll have to go back, before they miss me,' she said finally.

Diem had been sprawled out on the ledge but he sat up abruptly as soon as she spoke and grabbed her arm. 'What happens next?' he said sharply. 'How do I get *off* this island?'

'*I* don't know!' she replied, knocking his hand away. He didn't reply, but she could see the renewed anxiety in his face, shining dully in the green gloom. 'I'll think of something,' she said. Having won his trust, and brought him this far, she felt totally responsible for him now.

Jackie stood up. 'You've got to stay here. I'll bring some food.' And with that she dived into the pool. She surfaced carefully, lifting just her head out of the water first while she studied the beach. It was deserted, so she stood up, waded ashore and disappeared at once into the bush.

She took a short-cut back, using the trick that Greg had taught her, running a hundred paces, then walking a hundred to conserve energy, but even so she was out of breath by the time she could see the buildings ahead through the trees. She kept away from the family part of the Resort, because her hair was still wet, and she didn't want any awkward questions. Charlie and Sally would probably be out searching, and Greg wouldn't even notice, but you couldn't put anything over Mary. Best to give herself an excuse. She made her way to the pool, and dived in, gliding underwater until her momentum was exhausted, then surfacing and swimming with a relaxed stroke, arms and legs moving in perfect co-ordination. Jackie swam almost every day, and it showed.

At the other end she climbed out and padded across the tiles, picked up a towel that was draped over a table, threw it over her head and began to dry her hair energetically, her mind on the tricky problem of Diem's food. It would be easy to get some from the kitchen, and then she'd have to wrap it up well in plastic or. . . .

Suddenly two strong hands gripped her firmly from behind, pinning her arms to her sides. It didn't hurt, but she couldn't move.

'Surprise, surprise!' said a voice, and at the same time the towel was whipped away. Jackie spun around, and her face lit up with delight 'Uncle Andrew!' she cried.

SIX

Greg and Sally were equally surprised to see their uncle when the searchers trooped into the guest lounge, footsore, famished, and empty handed, later in the afternoon. 'G'day Uncle Andrew!' called Greg, running across to shake his hand.

Sally was close behind. 'Uncle Andrew! Great to see you!' she said, giving him a big kiss. 'How long are you staying?'

'As long as I'm welcome,' said Andrew Wilson, looking directly at his older brother.

Charlie didn't share the kids' enthusiasm. 'Hardly worth unpacking,' he said, and he wasn't joking.

Andrew chose to ignore the insult. 'It's good to see you haven't lost your sense of humour, Charlie,' he smiled. There was an awkward pause while they stood there, looking each other up and down.

Physically, the two men were poles apart. Andrew was slightly taller and eight years younger than Charlie, but much softer and less robust-looking with his fashionably casual clothes, finely chiselled features, immaculate black hair and pale, unblemished skin. Charlie, on the other hand, was tanned, and lean, and hard, his muscles rippling underneath his sweat-soaked singlet and jeans, his brown hair blonded in places by prolonged exposure to salt water and sun. Despite his fatigue, he exuded fitness and vitality.

'Jackie tells me you've got a manhunt going on,' said Andrew at last.

'That's right,' Charlie replied gruffly, then turned and made his way out on to the verandah. His mind was in a whirl. Things were getting a bit out of hand; first their money worries, then this damned business with Vo Diem (which he never should have let Jackie talk him into), then David Lee's offer to buy the island, and now, to top it all off, Andrew! Trust *him* to show up at the worst possible time! But then, Charlie reflected regretfully, *any* time was the wrong time as far as his younger brother was concerned. They'd never been close; not just because of the age gap, but because fundamentally, as people, they were as different as chalk and cheese.

Both had been born on Butterfly, growing up with the Great Barrier Reef at their back door, but that was about the only thing they had in common. In fact, their attitudes towards the Reef reflected the differences in their personalities perhaps better than anything else. To Charlie it had always been a place of constant interest, wonder, beauty, and delight. To Andrew it had been a resource, one to be *used*, and as a boy he had combed it for shells and bits of coral which he'd sold to tourists at outrageous prices, much to their father's dismay. But Old Man Wilson had been a realist; he had seen that Andrew was bright, enterprising, restless, forever searching for something new. Butterfly Island's horizons were too close, too confining, for him.

When their father died, he left eighty per cent of Butterfly to Charlie. Bitterly disappointed with his minor share, Andrew had left the island almost at once, going first to Brisbane, then Sydney, where he worked for a firm of accountants by day, studying at night. Then he'd begun to change jobs frequently, moving around, gaining experience, wheeling and dealing, learning all the time, and finally he'd gone out on his own, building a very successful investment business in a ʾw short years. He was still expanding in leaps and bounds and was an extremely wealthy man now.

Charlie had mixed feelings about the way things had gone; Andrew had been virtually forced on to the mainland, and it had been the making of him, just as their father had intended. But in personal terms the price had been perhaps too high; two brothers divided, with a gulf between them that would probably never be bridged. He smiled sadly to himself; *he* still had Butterfly Island, but for how much longer could he hang on? It didn't bear thinking about.

Charlie glanced up at the sky. It was overcast now, and the surface of the lagoon was disturbed and slate grey. The hot, humid atmosphere wrapped itself around him like a sweaty blanket, making everything an effort; even thinking.

He spotted Michelle Kim and Luong sitting by themselves at the end of the verandah, and they looked up expectantly as he walked over to join them. It was obvious from the empty glasses on the table that they'd been waiting for some time. 'No luck yet, Miss Kim,' he said, pulling up a chair. 'You'd better tell Mr Luong it may be necessary for him to stay the night.'

'I see,' said Michelle. As she explained the position to Diem's uncle in rapid Vietnamese, Mary came up with drinks on a tray. She put a glass down in front of Charlie, then reached over and began to clear the empties away. 'Can I get you another drink?' she asked when Michelle had finished translating, but the interpreter shook her head. 'Do you really believe Diem's trying to get to Indonesia?' Mary went on, wiping the plastic table top with a cloth.

Charlie sat up. 'Indonesia? What's all this about?' he asked. It was obvious Mary and Michelle had been doing a bit of talking during the long afternoon.

'There was never direct proof that his parents' boat was lost at sea,' Michelle explained. 'There is a remote chance they are alive; maybe in a refugee camp.'

'Can't the Government check that out?' asked Charlie.

Michelle smiled slightly. 'We try, Mr Wilson, but these things take time, especially when there is another country involved.'

Charlie understood her problem. 'I've had a taste of bureaucracy myself, Miss Kim,' he said. 'I can see why the kid's going it alone.'

Michelle's brow wrinkled. 'My worry is the risks Diem is taking, Mr Wilson. Hiding on that plane, for example. If he is not found soon, who knows?' Jackie came up as Michelle spoke, and Charlie felt her hand on his shoulder, looked up, and acknowledged her presence with a brief smile.

There was silence then; Miss Kim's words had given them all something to contemplate, and while Charlie was worried, Jackie was downright scared. She didn't say anything, but stood beside her father, thinking of Diem, alone in the cave. His life lay in her hands. If she took him food, and helped him to get off the island, he'd have another go at reaching his parents, of that there was no doubt; and maybe this time he wouldn't be so lucky; maybe this time he'd be serioiusly hurt, perhaps even killed. And it would be her fault. She shuddered. On the other hand, if she dobbed him in, his uncle would take him back to Brisbane and he'd never get another chance. What was she going to *do*?

'OK, everyone! Break's over. We don't want to run out of light, do we?' Sergeant Connolly's powerful voice broke into her thoughts and she turned to see him coming down the verandah with Uncle Andrew and Greg, his big boots crunching on the concrete.

'Anything I can do?' asked Andrew.

'Not at the moment,' replied Charlie stiffly, moving off. Andrew stood watching as his brother followed Greg and the policeman across the lawn, and then he noticed Jackie, standing to one side, serious, subdued, and alone.

'Aren't you searching, Jackie?' he asked brightly.

She jumped. 'What?' she blurted out. 'Oh! Sure,' and ran off with a guilty grin.

She could have overtaken them quickly, because they were only a short distance ahead, but she lagged behind, a thousand and one possibilities and consequences racing through her mind. Finally, by the time the searchers emerged on to the beach, she had decided what she was going to do.

'Dad, wait!' she called.

Charlie stopped and turned around. 'What, Jackie?' he said impatiently as she ran to catch up.

'I didn't *mean* to do the wrong thing,' she said.

Charlie's eyes narrowed. 'What are you talking about?'

'Diem trusted me,' she continued excitedly, 'But I heard what Miss Kim said and she's right. Because he's desperate he might try anything!'

He put a comforting hand on her shoulder. 'Calm down, love. Tell me what you're on about.'

Jackie took a deep breath. 'I know where Diem is,' she said.

After the searchers left, Andrew went back inside and asked Mary to find him a room, where he lost no time in stepping into a cooling shower. Afterwards, as he rubbed himself down, he frowned at the apparent inability of the towel to dry his skin properly in the humid air, and by the time he had put on his beautifully cut, open-necked sports shirt, matching slacks, and an expensive pair of casual shoes, he was as hot and uncomfortable as he'd been before he'd stepped into the shower. He smiled grimly: he'd forgotten just how oppressive the tropical weather could be.

Wandering back into the lounge in search of another drink, he saw Sally behind the counter at Reception. 'Holding the fort?' he asked.

She smiled. 'Something like that.'

He leaned forward confidentially. 'Is it my imagination, or is your Dad grumpier than usual?'

Sally laughed. 'It's hard to tell with Dad, except when *you're* here. What did you do when you were kids? Beat each other up?'

Andrew smiled. 'We took turns.' He looked around the deserted lounge. 'Even allowing for juvenile runaways, there's a distinct air of gloom about the place.'

Sally nodded agreement. 'Bookings are down again,' she replied. 'The island's in worse trouble than it was last year. It's pretty frustrating.'

'Is that a personal opinion?' asked Andrew, watching her shrewdly.

Sally grunted. 'My ideas don't exactly match Dad's,' she said, tossing her head.

'Neither did *mine*,' said Andrew. 'I don't expect he'll see sense this time, either.'

'What about?' asked Sally curiously.

Her uncle smiled. 'Be fair, Sal. I may only have twenty per cent of this island, but I'm entitled to have my say when there's a million dollars at stake.'

Her jaw dropped '*A million dollars?*'

Andrew nodded. 'David Lee's offer to buy the island.' He paused for a moment, studying her incredulous face. 'You mean your father hasn't *told* you?'

She shook her head. 'No, not yet,' she said quietly.

By the time the searchers reached the beach above the cave where Jackie had left Vo Diem it was very late in the afternoon. Heavy clouds scudded low over the grey, restlessly-heaving sea and the coconut trees were tossing uneasily in the wind. It was a depressing scene which suited Jackie's mood. She stood a little apart from the other searchers as they all stared expectantly into the sea above the entrance to the underwater cave. Jackie bit her lip. Her father was down there, and when he came up, he'd have Vo Diem. She knew she'd done the right thing, but she felt a real rat, just the same, because Diem had trusted her. She didn't know how she was going to look him in the face.

But she didn't have to, because when Charlie emerged from the sea he was alone. He strode up the beach, and stood before them, hands on hips, his swimming trunks accentuating his muscular, deeply-tanned physique. 'Gone,' he said, gritting his teeth.

'*Wonderful*.' said Sergeant Connolly sarcastically. 'We'll have to comb the bush again. I don't suppose *you'd* like to tell my Inspector?'

Charlie glared at Jackie. 'It looks like your young friend didn't trust you after all,' he said angrily. She opened her mouth to protest but he silenced her at once. 'Go home!' he barked, and then turned his back and strode away along the beach. The others followed. Alone, tears streaming down her cheeks, Jackie watched them for a minute, then began to trudge back towards the Resort.

For a while Greg, Charlie and the Sergeant walked in silence, each, in his own way, frustrated and annoyed. Charlie was angry with Jackie for taking matters into her own hands; thanks to her interference they'd lost a whole day. The policeman was concerned about his report; this kid was beginning to make him look damn silly! Greg, for his part, was annoyed with himself. He'd known about the cave; why hadn't it occurred to *him* that Vo Diem might have been holed up there? What a dummy! He struck out savagely with his foot, throwing up a shower of sand.

Finally, Charlie spoke. 'I should've thought of the cave myself,' he said to Connolly. The policeman made no comment so Charlie went on. 'Mind you,' he said, as if to excuse himself, 'how was I to know that someone would give him a guided tour?'

Trudging along beside his father, Greg winced. Boy,

was Jackie going to cop it when they got home!

The beach ended abruptly in a spray-shrouded, rocky point, forcing them to climb a perilous ascent up giant, spray-soaked, slippery boulders. The light was very poor now, and as they rested at the top, Charlie cast an anxious eye at the weather. He couldn't see the mainland mountains now, and the horizon was drawing in, the islands disappearing, one by one, behind a curtain of heavy rain. A couple of kilometres away across the channel, Beacon Island became indistinct, then disappeared as the squall raced across the water, and soon he could actually see the rain, spearing down into the heaving sea; he felt a few drops, then the downpour was upon them, hissing on to the rocks, driving sharp, then running warm and liquid on his bare skin.

'Charlie!' Connolly, already wet through, was crouching over a sandy patch between some rocks, examining a set of footprints. 'He's not bothering to cover his tracks any more,' the policeman said from beneath his dripping hat. 'We're close.'

Spurred on by their discovery, they followd the trail to the next bay, and as they emerged on to the beach they found something else; Vo Diem's shirt, lying on the clean white sand; and beyond, another set of footprints, rapidly eroding in the pouring rain. They led down to the water. Another hoax?

Sergeant Connolly knelt and examined them: it wasn't; the tracks were one way with no signs of doubling back; the kid had really walked into the sea. 'What's all this about?' he asked looking up at Charlie. 'Another cave?'

Charlie shook his head. 'Not here.'

Connolly stood up. 'Little fool!' he said. 'It looks like he's trying to swim to one of the other islands!'

Charlie looked out across the turbulent, rain-swept bay. 'He's got no hope,' he said. 'We'd better go back and get the *Elizabeth*. In a sea like that he hasn't got a chance!'

'Forget it, Charlie,' the policeman said.

Charlie glanced at him sharply. 'What? You're not *calling off* the search?'

Connolly nodded. 'You'd be wasting your time.'

'But there's a fifty per cent chance that the kid's alive!'

'Fifty per cent?'

'He's a survivor, Pat.'

The policeman shook his head. 'If you want to take your boat out there and look for him, good luck to you, mate,' he said. 'I don't like it any more than you do but you can't see more than fifty metres.' He squinted at the sky through the driving rain before going on. 'If I were you I'd get back and batten down the hatches.'

Charlie gritted his teeth. Connolly was right. 'As if the kid hasn't got enough against him,' he said.

Forty-five minutes later they were back at the Resort, to the news that Cyclone Gene was bearing down upon them from the Coral Sea with torrential rain and wind gusts of over a hundred and fifty kilometres-an-hour. The area up and down the coast from Ellis River was on official Cyclone Alert — the warning had come through on the radio while they were out.

Charlie wasn't surprised. All the signs had been there, and it was the right time of year. December through to April was the cyclone season; when the giant, capricious storms were born in the warm tropic seas. Sometimes they came to nothing, and bothered no one, losing intensity and fizzling out before they reached the coast. But at other times they passed over the offshore islands and coastal towns of northern Australia leaving a train of devastation, and sometimes death, behind them.

As soon as Mary gave them the news, Pat Connolly

left for Ellis River in the police launch, taking Michelle Kim and Luong with him. It would be a rough trip, but the Sergeant had to go: he'd be needed on the mainland tonight.

After the pitching boat had disappeared into the rain, Charlie made his way back to the guest Lounge. The wind had become noticeably stronger now: it was moaning through the coconut trees bending them before it, occasionally ripping off a frond to send it whirling through the air. Charlie wasn't particularly worried: Butterfly Island Resort had been designed and built with the cyclone season in mind. It wasn't cyclone-proof but it went pretty close. The guest cabins all had storm shutters, but as the cabins were spread up and down the beach they were not the safest place to be in a one hundred and fifty kilometre-an-hour storm! When a cyclone approached it was routine procedure to bring all the guests into the Lounge, which was extra-solidly built. Then, with everybody safely under one roof they could close it down tight and sit out the worst of the storm with food, water, first aid, and radio close at hand.

The whole family was in Reception, listening to the radio. Sometimes cyclones changed course and veered away at the last minute; but not this one. The news wasn't good. Gene was expected to pass over Butterfly Island and cross the coast at about one o'clock. They were in for it tonight!

'All right, no panic, no mistakes,' said Charlie. 'You all know what has to be done.'

'Where do you want me, Charlie?' asked Andrew.

'Work with Greg,' his brother replied. 'Storm shutters first. Let's go.'

As Jackie and Sally headed off to carry out their pre-arranged tasks inside, Andrew followed Greg out into the rain. They were soaked to the skin before they reached the first guest house, but at least it was warm, even in the howling wind. Greg knocked on the door, explained the position, and asked the occupants to move to the Lounge for the night. Then he began to show his uncle how to lower the storm shutters and lock them down; but Andrew Wilson had been through it all before, and by the time he and Greg reached the third guest house they were working as a well-drilled team.

As they worked, they talked, and Andrew made the most of the opportunity. 'Still want to fly planes when you grow up?' he asked Greg, as they slid a shutter into place.

'You bet!' the boy replied.

'A job like that takes a lot of training, you know,' said Andrew, 'and that costs money.'

Greg knew what his uncle was getting at: it was money that they didn't have. 'Plenty of time yet,' he said cheerfully. 'Dad'll work something out.'

They arrived at the last house, and Greg didn't bother knocking on the door because the unit was unoccupied. 'Why do you and Dad always growl at each other?' he asked, as he reached up for the shutter.

Andrew grinned. 'Be fair, mate. *Charlie* does the growling.'

'Yair, but you stir him up,' said Greg, slamming the protective covering down.

'The decision I had to make is the same one you'll face sooner or later, Greg,' said Andrew seriously. 'Even a piece of paradise like Butterfly can start to look like a dead end. . . .' His voice trailed off, and Greg looked around to see Charlie standing on the path, wiping the rain out of his eyes with the back of his hand.

'Storm shutters are up,' said Andrew, changing the subject. 'Where do you want us now; wharf or work-shop?'

'I'll see to the wharf,' Charlie replied. He looked at his brother hard. 'You're enjoying this, aren't you?' he said accusingly.

'Come on Charlie, I'm not stupid. I understand the danger,' Andrew replied, and then he grinned. 'But on the other hand, it brings back a few memories!'

Recollections of cyclones past were flooding back on Charlie, too. They were good memories; memories of dangers shared; memories of two boys, working and laughing together in the wind and rain long ago. Suddenly he realised that he still liked his brother a lot, and he hoped that the feeling was mutual. He grinned back.

'Do cyclones scare you, Uncle Andrew?' asked Greg, as they made their way to the workshop.

Andrew evaded the question. 'Your grandfather used to say that a good storm was God's way of reminding us not to get smart,' he replied with a smile. The answer satisfied Greg, and they set to work collecting outdoor furniture, rubbish bins, and anything else that could possibly become a wind-borne missile, stacking it all inside the workshop. Finally the job appeared to be done. 'Is that the lot?' asked Andrew.

'Just my surf-ski,' replied Greg, pointing to the streamlined fibreglass shape lying on the sand. 'I can stow that.'

'Right,' said his uncle. 'Lock up when you've finished. I want to double-check those shutters.' He tossed a padlock to Greg and then he was gone, struggling to make headway against the howling wind.

As Greg dragged his ski inside Charlie came running up from the jetty. 'I need a hand, son,' he panted. 'Help me drag the outboards further up the sand.' Greg laid the ski down on the concrete floor and followed his father at once. Behind him the workshop door, unlocked, banged to and fro.

By the time Andrew, Charlie and Greg arrived back at the main building, the Lounge had been transformed. Jackie and Sally had dragged sleeping bags into a space

110

in the centre of the room, and Mary was filling half-a-dozen hurricane lanterns with kerosene. There were torches on the Reception counter, with a box of spare batteries. Music was playing from a transistor radio on the shelf; the local radio station at Ellis River would stay on the air all night to give the latest reports on Cyclone Gene. Most of the guests had arrived, and were standing about apprehensively, not quite sure what to expect. Charlie smiled to himself; from some of the expressions, you'd think the end of the world had come!

Suddenly the door burst open and another guest, a girl of about Sally's age, staggered into the room holding her head. Mary hurried across. 'What happened?' she asked urgently.

'Tree branch,' muttered the girl, taking her hand away so that Mary could see her wound. 'I guess I didn't duck in time.'

'It's not serious,' Mary reassured her. 'But I'll put something on it just the same.'

As she reached for the first-aid kit Charlie stepped into the centre of the room. 'Anything loose out there goes like a bullet,' he announced. 'So from now on, everybody please stay inside. Are we all here?' Sally had been counting, and as she nodded confirmation he breathed a sigh of relief. The room was not even crowded; thank heavens the Resort wasn't heavily booked.

Jackie was looking around too, but her thoughts were far from comforting; all were present except one: she wondered sadly what Vo Diem was doing now.

After a while everyone found a place and tried to settle down, listening uneasily as the noise increased. The moaning of the wind rose to a howl, then a roar, and then a loud, continuous shriek, punctuated by sudden, sharp metallic bangs just above their heads as unseen, wind-borne debris impacted with the galvanised iron roof. The fronds of a tortured palm played a weird tattoo against an outside wall, and the rain still came drumming down. Jackie could picture the fury raging outside: the trees would be bent over until their topmost branches were nearly touching the ground; the rain would be driving along almost horizontally before the wind; the waves would be rearing up out of the blackness and eating into their beach, dragging the sand back into the stormy sea. She shuddered and snuggled further into her sleeping bag.

Suddenly there was a loud crash just above their heads. The room shuddered and the lights went out. Jackie sat bolt upright. Almost at once she heard Charlie's voice, calm and reassuring in the darkness. 'That has to be a tree branch,' he said. There was the flare of a match followed by a soft, warm glow, illuminating Mary's face as she lit a hurricane lamp, then another one, and another, and in no time the darkness was relieved by moving pools of yellow light as Greg and Sally carried the lanterns, distributing them around the room. Jackie sank back and closed her eyes with relief.

After all the lamps were handed out, Greg, Sally, Charlie and Andrew met back at the Reception counter. Mary had been listening to the radio, holding it up to her ear to overcome the noise of the wind. 'It's heading right for us,' she announced. 'They say it'll cross the coast at about half-past two.'

Charlie looked at his watch. Half-past ten. Four hours to go. Things would get worse before they got better! As if on cue there was an ominous creaking in the roof, and all eyes immediately became riveted on the ceiling.

'I bet this wind could rip it right off,' said Greg.

'If you can't say something optimistic, keep it to yourself!' ordered Charlie. 'We'll do *fine*!' He forced a smile and looked around. 'It's the first time we've had the whole family together for a long time.'

Sally spoke. 'True, Dad. It's a *perfect* opportunity to discuss Mr Lee's offer to buy the island.'

Charlie's jaw dropped. How did *she* know about *that*? *Andrew*! He cast a furious look in his brother's direction.

Andrew shrugged. 'I assumed she knew,' he said.

'How did *you* know?' Charlie snapped.

'I'm a shareholder too, you know,' Andrew returned evenly. 'Or maybe you've forgotten?'

Charlie ignored the sarcasm. 'Well,' he said, 'there's nothing to discuss. Money can't buy this island, and that's that!'

But that wasn't good enough for Sally. 'I want to know why you didn't tell us,' she said.

'The decision was made. What was the point?' Charlie replied. She waited, still not satisfied. Charlie caught his breath. She looked very beautiful in the soft lamp-light; Sally was growing up. 'All right,' he said. 'I kept it to myself because a million dollars sounds like a lot of money, and I didn't want to give Lee the satisfaction of causing trouble in my family. Of course, I might've *known* who would turn up!' He gave Andrew another dirty look.

'But we don't really *own* the island, do we?' Sally asked.

Charlie snorted. 'What are you talking about?'

'What about the second mortgage with the bank?'

He was surprised: he didn't know she knew about *that*. 'So, we owe the bank money: who doesn't?' he said.

'But suppose we couldn't make the payments?' Sally went on. 'The bank could legally take the island away from us, couldn't it?'

Charlie looked at her open-mouthed, not quite sure how to answer, but the storm saved him further embarrassment. There was a sudden racket at one of the windows, as if thousands of people were standing outside, throwing pebbles at the glass. Charlie snapped on a torch.

It was a terrifying sight. One set of shutters had gone; Fragments of torn timber flapped pitifully on a twisted hinge, and the unprotected glass was bowing ominously inwards as the wind drove the rain against it with prodigious force, the water staying there after impact, momentarily supported by the blast, before streaming away in sheets. There wasn't a moment to lose, because the window could give way at any second, and then they'd really be in trouble.

As Charlie moved towards the door, Greg jumped up, too. 'I'll help, Dad!' he called.

'You stay in here!' Charlie snapped. He stuck a hammer in his belt, grabbed a handful of nails, and picked up the planks that he'd set aside for just this purpose. Then he saw Andrew waiting beside the door, and acknowledged his brother's presence with a brief nod. He wouldn't say so, but he was glad to have him.

'Ready?' Andrew asked. Charlie nodded again, and his brother took a firm grip on the handle and opened the door.

Outside, the roar of the gale was unbelievable. The wind snatched at the planks in Charlie's arms, threatening to blow him away, and it took the combined strength of both men to reach the window and nail them in place over the glass. As they worked they could see the watery images of frightened faces watching them from inside.

'You've really done a job on Sally, haven't you?' Charlie yelled above the blast.

'Don't be stupid!' Andrew shouted back. 'The girl does the office work. She knows what's going on!'

'Just keep *out* of it, Andrew!' warned Charlie, spitting water as he delivered the final hammer blow.

They made their way inside to welcome cups of coffee, and Charlie, dry again, went across to Sally, alone in her pool of lantern light. 'You were right,' he said, sitting down beside her, 'I should've told you all about the offer.'

She looked at him sadly. 'Do you think I *want* you to sell the island?' she asked.

'You tell *me*.'

'Jackie and Greg don't know the business side of things,' she went on, 'but I do. Every year, our bookings get fewer. We can't borrow the money to put your plans into action, not even enough for a decent advertising campaign.'

'Facts and figures aren't everything, Sal,' countered Charlie. 'We can hang in there, as long as the family works as a team.'

Sally wouldn't accept that. 'Facts and figures mean this much, Dad. When the time comes and we can't pay the bank, they'll take Butterfly and leave us with nothing. Right now, it's worth a *million*.'

Charlie shook his head. 'Your mother and I had great plans for this island,' he said softly, 'and I promised her that I'd make it all happen.'

'Would she hold you to that now, Dad?' Sally asked, meeting his eyes.

Charlie avoided her gaze, and glanced across at Andrew, who was playing cards with Greg. His jaw hardened. 'Your *uncle*'s been talking to you!' he said, accusingly.

Sally slowly shook her head. 'I do my own thinking, Dad. Give me credit for that.'

Charlie smiled. 'I'll give you credit for a lot more. The last seven years I couldn't have run this place without you.'

'You'll *have to*, soon.'

The full meaning behind her words slammed home like a blow from a sledgehammer. Sally, *leaving*? Charlie gaped. Maybe he hadn't heard her correctly; but one glance at her face told him the awful truth.

She shrugged. 'There's nothing for me here any more, Dad. I'm not going to stay and watch this island go down the drain.'

'You can't go! exclaimed Charlie. 'You're just a *kid*!'

'I'll be eighteen in a few months,' replied Sally quietly. 'I'm sorry, but for the first time since Mum died, I've got to think about *me*.'

Vo Diem was scared. The whole world seemed to be filled with noise, flying missiles and stinging rain. The wind was a solid force, tearing at his body, threatening to knock him off his legs and blow him away. He groped through the darkness, not quite sure where he was or where he was going, staggering, crouching low so as to offer the least resistance to the gale. There was a constant deluge of falling coconuts, and time and again he heard fronds ripping from the palm trees somewhere in the darkness above him. He flung himself to the ground, arms up to protect his head as the heavy branches came crashing down around him. Once a whole tree fell only metres away, unseen in the blackness, thudding into the sodden ground with sickening force. Diem's survival instinct told him that sooner or later he was going to be in the wrong place at the wrong time when something fell. He had to find shelter, and soon!

Suddenly he became aware of a glow ahead. The Resort! He stumbled on through the rain, and soon he could make out the silhouetted buildings, with warm orange light spilling through the chinks in the shuttered windows. He ran across and flattened himself against a wall, held there by the force of the breeze. He rested for a moment, catching his breath, then edged his way along to one of the windows and tried to peer inside, but his view was obscured by the shutter. He felt for the bolt, slid it back, and began to lift the heavy wooden frame.

Instantly the wind took charge. With a groan of tortured metal the shutter was torn from its hinges and swept away, crashing against the side of the building before disappearing into the rain-swept gloom. For a brief moment Diem could see into the room, and there, staring straight back at him was the watery image of Jackie's wide-eyed, frightened face. He heard her scream, even above the storm, and then the glass gave way before the onslaught of wind and rain, showering her with fragments. She screamed once more and he turned and ran.

He could hear men's voices behind him, raised in alarm, but soon they were swallowed up in the cyclone's roar as he ran back into the darkness. And then he heard something else: a slamming sound, repeated at irregular intervals, as if some demented soul were opening and closing a door. It *was* a door! The workshop! He could see it now, just ahead, the door swinging wildly, its massive old hinges somehow withstanding the fury of the gale. A haven at last! He slipped inside and with a superhuman effort pulled the door closed behind him.

The interior of the workshop was pitch black. Diem picked his way through the darkness, blundering several times into mysterious objects. Feeling around like a blind man, he was able to identify the hard cold shape of a rubbish bin, and then some outdoor furniture. Suddenly there was a flash of light outside. A torch, playing on the unshuttered window! Instinctively Diem dived for cover behind a row of shelves and waited, heart racing. The light left the window, then reappeared at the narrow crack beneath the door. He heard the rattle of the handle, and then the workshop was flooded with light as the door was opened, then closed again with difficulty against the storm. Footsteps approached on the concrete floor, then stopped and the torch swept systematically around the room. He shrank back further behind the shelves and waited for the challenge that would mean discovery, but the words didn't come. All he could hear was the pounding of his heart and the cyclone's roar, then the door opened and closed again and the light was gone. Once more he was alone. He crawled from his hiding place and blundered through the darkness to the door. Time to go, storm or no storm! But the door wouldn't budge. The person with the torch, whoever it had been, had locked it from the outside! Dispirited, Vo Diem sank to the floor, a prisoner once more.

All eyes were on Charlie as he came back into the Lounge, wet through. 'You left the workshop unlocked,' he said to Greg.

'Crikey!' exclaimed Greg. 'I must have forgot! I was just about to do it when you yelled at me about the outboards and . . .'

'Forget it,' smiled Charlie, giving him a consoling pat on the shoulder. 'Forget it. No harm done.' He looked across to the broken window. Andrew had nailed a card table across the opening, and Sally was busy sweeping up the broken glass. 'Everything seems to be under control here,' he said. Andrew gave him an exaggerated 'thumbs-up' sign, but Charlie ignored him and walked over to Jackie, sitting expectantly in the corner of the room. 'Feeling a bit better now?' he asked, crouching down beside her.

'I'm OK, Dad,' she said. 'Did you . . . did you . . .?'

Charlie shook his head. 'I didn't see *anyone* out there, love,' he said gently. 'I wish I had.'

'But I *saw* him, Dad!' Jackie protested. 'I'm sure I saw him.'

'I think your imagination's playing tricks,' he replied. 'It's a rough night, we're all on edge. . . .'

'It was *Diem*!'

Charlie stood up. 'Curl up, and try to get some sleep,' he said firmly. 'That's an order.' And there was something in his voice that told Jackie it would be unwise indeed not to obey.

Vo Diem blundered about the shed, searching for another way out. The window offered a distinct possibility, but it was locked, and he groped around in the darkness trying to find something with which to break the glass. He felt an object leaning against a wall; something long, and hard, and smooth, and stream-lined. A surf-ski! A paddle too, and a life-jacket, lying on the floor nearby. At once a plan began to form in his mind: a suicidal plan, in this storm, but a plan, nevertheless.

Picking up the ski he held it above his head and used it like a battering ram to break the window. No need to worry about the noise. He slid the sleek shape through the opening, tossed the paddle and jacket out after it, and then climbed through the window himself, taking care not to cut himself on the jagged edges of broken glass. Outside he paused for a moment to don the jacket, and then picked up the ski, only to have the wind snatch it roughly from his arms and send it crashing against the workshop wall. He tried dragging it along the ground with more success, and headed off towards the beach.

Diem heard the waves long before he could see them, and even when he eventually emerged on to the beach the sea itself was still invisible, lost in the darkness and the flying spray. But he could feel the sand shuddering as the waves broke, the foam that marked their destruction gleaming dully and briefly at his feet before being sucked back into the seething gloom. There was no shelter now, and he crouched in the teeth of the gale, in the dark, trying to peer through the rain and the spray and the wind-borne sand in an attempt to assess the dangers that were all the more terrifying because they were largely unseen. Diem's heart missed a beat. It would be sheer madness, *suicide*, to go out in *that*! But then he thought of the alternatives . . . captivity, confinement, with all chance of finding his parents gone.

He took a deep breath, stood up, and dragged the ski quickly down the sand.

He lasted quite a while, sustained by a natural sense of balance and a desperate will to survive. He just hung on, paddling hard all the time, trying to keep the surf-ski headed into the sea. He could sense, rather than see a wave coming. The ski would drop, then rocket violently upwards, and he would be surrounded by water that tugged at his body, threatening to drag him over sideways. But somehow, he managed to right the ski again, and then he would be in the clear, paddling furiously before the next onslaught.

After a while it all became automatic, and his mind, numbed by fear and fatigue, began to turn to other things. He was in another ocean, in another storm, far away. Waves were battering a small boat, pitifully small, hopelessly overloaded with refugees. A huge wave broke over the deck, snatching a small child from its mother's arms and carrying it into the heaving sea. He saw his parents, clinging together on the pitching deck. He cried out 'Mother! Father!' but his words were snatched away by the wind. Another wave towered above him. It broke.

He was rolling over and over. The surging foam closed over him. It was darker than ever. He couldn't breathe. And that was the last he knew. . . .

SEVEN

Jackie slept late the next morning, after a restless night haunted by dreams of Vo Diem. When finally she opened her eyes sunlight was streaming in through the windows. She sat up and looked around. The shutters had been removed, the guests were gone, and Greg was helping Sally put the hurricane lanterns away. 'Trust *you* to sleep in,' he said, looking down at her. Jackie pouted and lay down again.

'Hello, young Jack. Welcome back to the land of the living,' said Uncle Andrew cheerily. He and Charlie were examining the shattered window. The card table, its role of makeshift shutter over, was leaning against the wall.

'You look a bit better than you did last night,' smiled Charlie.

'The storm's gone?' muttered Jackie, not quite able to believe it, still not quite awake.

'And nightmares with it, I hope,' Charlie grinned. Cyclone Gene had crossed the coast during the early hours, as predicted, and had moved inland. There, cut off from its energy source, the sea, it had weakened rapidly and was now a spent force.

'Breakfast in ten minutes, Charlie!' called Mary from the family-room.

'We'll do the rounds first!' Charlie called back. 'I won't have any appetite until I know what the damage is.'

121

Andrew went with him. They were prepared for the worst, but a quick walk round the Resort brought relief. A number of trees had come down, and the ground was littered with palm fronds, fallen coconuts, and other assorted debris, but apart from one or two broken windows, Butterfly Island had stood up well to the onslaught of wind and rain. The beach was eroded in places, scoured by the waves, but the sand would come back, given time. The dinghies were intact, lined up in a neat row above high-water mark; the jetty was still rock-solid on its piles, and the *Elizabeth* was moored alongside, undamaged.

'It's a miracle!' said Andrew, hands on hips, surveying the scene.

Charlie nodded. 'A bit of luck, but mostly good management. Credit where credit's due.'

'True,' agreed Andrew. 'Cyclone nil, Wilsons one. Dad made this place to last.' He glanced at his brother. 'Got your appetite back?' Charlie nodded again and they began to walk back towards the house.

'Sally told me last night that she wants to leave,' said Charlie.

Andrew thought carefully before he replied. This was a sensitive issue. 'Haven't you been expecting it?' he asked at last. 'She's not a little girl any more, you know.'

Charlie stopped walking. 'I *wasn't* expecting it,' he said flatly. 'Is she moving to Sydney?'

'If you're suggesting that I influenced her . . .' protested Andrew.

'Well, you're always talking about life in the big city,' accused Charlie.

'She's *changing*, Charlie,' replied his brother. 'You've got to change too, or you'll lose everything.'

Charlie saw red. 'You've got the money to bail me out; even to get my plans moving!'

Andrew shook his head. 'I won't throw good money after bad. The problems are straightforward, Charlie.

You've got the solution in your own hands. *Accept* David Lee's offer for the island!'

After breakfast, on Charlie's orders, Greg and Jackie went to the workshop and began to return the outdoor tables and chairs and umbrellas and rubbish bins to their proper places. There were leaves and palm fronds everywhere but, apart from the broken window, the ancient shed was still intact. It had withstood many a cyclone, and no doubt would survive many more in the years to come. They worked in silence, both well aware of just how lucky they had been.

When the job was done, Greg stood in the open doorway, scratching his head. 'My surf-ski's gone,' he said.

Jackie didn't reply. She was more interested in the broken window.

'I couldn't have left it on the *beach*,' Greg went on, more to re-assure himself than anything else.

'Didn't you stow it?' she asked absently, carefully gathering the glass fragments from the gound.

'I *thought* I did,' muttered Greg, unsure. 'But I *thought* I locked the workshop, too.' He shrugged unhappily, thinking of the door slamming to and fro in the cyclone. 'Dad'll *kill* me!'

Jackie stood up, her hand full of broken glass. 'Look at this,' she said. 'The glass has fallen on the *outside*.'

'So what?' said Greg bluntly.

'If the storm broke the glass, the fragments should be all on the *inside*,' she replied. Greg followed as she hurried into the workshop and crouched by the window on the other side. There was hardly any glass on the concrete floor. 'So how did the window get broken?' she asked, looking up at Greg.

'Probably because I left the door open,' he shrugged, not really interested. He was more concerned about his surf-ski. 'Come on, help me look.'

Jackie glanced around the room. 'Your paddle's missing, too,' she said.

Greg shook his head in dismay. 'Don't tell me I left *that* outside as well,' he groaned.

Jackie looked at him keenly. 'Someone might have taken it,' she said; and Greg knew exactly whom she had in mind. He thought *that* was a crazy idea, but he followed her, just the same, as she led the way along the beach to the spot where they'd found Vo Diem's shirt. 'I *did* see him last night,' Jackie declared.

'You *think* you did,' Greg countered.

'He never left the island,' she said.

Greg shook his head in exasperation. Jackie sure had a one-track mind! 'His tracks went straight down into the water, right here,' he said. 'There are no tracks coming back. What did he do, grow wings?'

She ignored him, looking around, trying to put herself in the Vietnamese boy's place, endeavouring to think as he must have done. She decided to re-trace his steps. She walked down to the water's edge and began to wade in, up to her ankles, then her knees, and then she stopped, feeling a little foolish. She turned back towards the shore.

'Give up?' taunted Greg.

Suddenly she had the answer! It had been there all the time, right before their eyes. 'Watch this!' she called triumphantly, and began to wade back, her legs churning up quite a wave as she headed for an old, dead tree that had fallen across the beach. The trunk extended from the bush right out into the water: perhaps a relic of a cyclone long past. Jackie climbed on to the trunk and, hands outstretched, one foot behind the other like an Olympic gymnast balancing on a beam, she used it as a walkway right to the edge of the bush. Reaching for an overhanging branch, she hauled herself up and off the log, then dropped lightly on to the grass. She had crossed the beach without stepping on the sand, leaving no trace! 'So that's how he did it,' Jackie said.

Greg was impressed, but Charlie was far from convinced when they both cornered him in the family-room a short time later.

'You imagined it, Jackie,' he said.

'But Dad, it *was* Diem last night, honest!' she protested. 'What about Greg's missing surf-ski? And the paddle? Please tell Sergeant Connolly so they can start searching again. *Please?*'

'Suppose Diem *was* on the island last night?' said Charlie. 'Suppose he *did* take the surf-ski? How long do you think he would have lasted out there?'

'Please Dad . . .'

'All right! All right!' exclaimed Charlie, raising both hands to silence her. 'I'll tell the Sergeant, but the rest is up to him. Until he lets us know, I don't want to hear any more about it! Understood?' Jackie nodded. Despite the evidence, despite her arguments, it was clear that she had pushed her father as far as he would go. In her opinion it wasn't far enough; not where a life was concerned, but the ball was in her court now. She left the room without another word, and made her way to the beach.

She stood on a high point, looking across the channel. There was only a short chop running now, and the sea sparkled in the sun, but last night, out there in the darkness and the wind and the rain, it had been a different story. It was difficult to believe that anyone could have survived. For a moment her confidence was shaken and she bit her lip as she gazed out over the sea. Maybe she was kidding herself. Maybe she was wrong. Maybe she *had* imagined seeing Vo Diem. There was one way to find out!

Jackie ran back to the house. Fortunately the office was empty, so she didn't have to invent excuses for being there. She rummaged through the drawers until she found the book of tide tables and a chart of Butterfly

Island and surrounding waters. Quickly she looked up the relevant date in the tide book, jotted down a few figures, then unrolled the chart on the top of the desk, placing a dictionary on one end and the Ellis River Telephone Directory on the other to hold it down flat. She bent to her task using parallel rulers and a pro-tractor and five minutes later she leaned back in the chair, a satisfied smile on her lips. She was no navigator, but she could read a compass and plot a basic course. The tides had been right last night, and the current had been favourable, and if Vo Diem had managed to survive the raging seas, according to her reckoning he should be . . . there! Her finger traced the pencil line that she had drawn lightly upon the chart, from Butterfly across the channel, and came to rest on nearby Beacon Island.

Although she had no means of knowing it, Jackie was right. At that very moment, three kilometres away, Vo Diem was lying semi-conscious on the sand of Beacon Island, still wearing the life-jacket that had saved his life. Of the surf-ski there was no sign. He stirred, sat up with difficulty and looked around. Scrubby trees grew right to the edge of the beach, and through their branches he could make out the white tower of a light-house, not far away. Diem climbed painfully to his feet and made his way cautiously towards it.

The bush was thick and the going tough, but soon he paused at the edge of the clearing that surrounded the base of the tower and looked up. The lighthouse loomed above him now, seeming to slide across the sky, until he realised that what *really* was moving was the scudding clouds. Apart from a few seagulls there was no sign of life, so he took his courage in both hands, broke cover, and walked boldly up to the door. It moved to his touch and he went inside, pulling it closed behind him.

The interior of the tower was quite roomy, with small windows, freshly-painted walls, and a clean concrete floor. A spiral staircase curved around the wall, leading up to the light twenty metres above his head. But it was the water that interested Vo Diem; a plastic bottle, full of it. He picked it up and drank greedily. Then he noticed the food: canned meat, soup, biscuits and jam, neatly packed in a cardboard box. There were two gas lamps, too, two rolled sleeping bags, and a radio, a powerful portable model. Somebody was camping on the island; probably two people. But where were they now?

Quickly Diem climbed the stairs, feeling giddy from hunger as well as vertigo as he circled round and round the tower walls. Eventually he emerged on to the top deck, and stood among the curiously-shaped lenses and mirrors of the automatic light, making a careful study of the ground below. From this height he could see the whole island. It was very small, only a few hundred metres long, and rather less across. There was no sign of the campers, and no boat drawn up on any of the beaches. Diem breathed a sigh of relief. It was obvious that the lighthouse was a base, but there was nobody else on the island now.

He lifted his eyes and a familiar sight came into view. Butterfly Island was just across the channel floating green and gold in the sparkling sea, seemingly so close he could reach out and touch it. Diem grinned wryly to himself. Last night in the darkness, before he lost consciousness, dry land, *any* dry land had seemed further away than the moon!

Forever an opportunist, he made the most of his windfall. It didn't take him long to find a way to open a few cans, and soon he was enjoying a hearty meal and listening to the radio. It was a local station, and he didn't like the music, but it was an unexpected luxury nonetheless, and as he ate Diem felt his spirits rising. He began to relax.

The music ended and a news bulletin began. Diem

was half-listening as he munched away, but suddenly he became very interested indeed. A fishing trawler had been stranded in Ellis River by the cyclone. Diem stopped chewing and listened carefully as the announcer's voice went on. The trawler was from Indonesia! She was called the *Sea Tiger* and was due to sail for home during the next two days as soon as her crew had made a few minor repairs. Vo Diem began to eat again with renewed vigour. This was the break he had been waiting for. He had to reach Ellis River somehow and get aboard that boat. But how? His mind began to spin without coming up with any useful ideas and he realised that he was very tired. Sleep now, worry about Ellis River and the *Sea Tiger* later. He turned the radio off, climbed the stairs, removed his life-jacket, and lay down in a secluded corner of the top deck. A minute later he was sound asleep.

Bob Gallio flew over to Butterfly from Ellis River later in the morning, and Sally, as usual, was waiting on the beach as the Buccaneer waddled up the sand. 'I worried about you last night,' said Bob, holding her close.

Sally snuggled in. 'We made it OK,' she said.

'I wish I could say the same,' returned Bob. 'We had two light planes damaged. Dad's done nothing but curse in Italian all morning.'

She looked up at him. 'I'm sorry,' she said.

'I hear you had hardly any damage at all,' went on Bob. 'Your Dad must be feeling relieved.'

'Not exactly,' said Sally.

'Why?'

'I told him I was going to move out.'

Bob was just as staggered as Charlie had been. 'Oh *brother*! How's he taking it?' he asked.

Sally grinned. 'He hasn't said much about it . . . yet!'

Bob left her then, and sought Charlie out. He found him in the Resort Office. 'Could I possibly speak to you for a minute, Mr Wilson?' he asked respectfully.

Charlie glanced up from his paperwork. 'Bob, if it's about your father's bill . . .'

'No. It's about Sally,' Bob interrupted. 'About her wanting to go away.'

'I think that's between me and Sally, don't you?'

'Not really.'

Charlie's eyes narrowed. This was a new Bob. 'What do you mean, not really?'

Bob shrugged. 'Well, *I'm* going to miss her, too.'

'If you don't mind, I'm busy.' Charlie looked down at his papers once again, but Bob stepped forward insistently.

'Please listen to what I've got to say, Mr Wilson.'

Wearily, Charlie leaned back in his chair. 'OK, Bob, I'm listening.'

Now that he had Charlie's attention, Bob didn't quite know how to begin. 'There's more to life than a tiny speck of sand surrounded by coral,' he said. 'Sally's got to see places, meet people, get some experience!'

'There's nothing out there to equal what she's got, *right here*, on Butterfly Island,' returned Charlie evenly.

'But how's she ever going to appreciate that if she doesn't go out and see for herself?' Bob was warming to his subject now but as far as Charlie was concerned the discussion was over.

'Yeah. Well, I'm sure you mean well, Bob,' he said.

'You didn't listen at all, Mr Wilson.'

'I *heard* what you *said*!' said Charlie emphatically.

'Then why are you keeping her here?' asked Bob.

That was enough for Charlie. 'You listen to me, young fella,' he growled, standing up. 'I told you before. This is a matter between me and my daughter. Now why don't you get in your little plane and go and run your errands like a good boy!'

Stung by the sarcasm, Bob could do nothing but watch as Charlie stormed from the room.

It was early evening before Diem awoke, to the glare of the light just above his head, the gas hissing, the mechanism clicking and whirring as the shutters turned, endlessly flashing the lighthouse's warning message out to sea. Diem climbed to his feet and looked around. The lights of Butterfly Island were twinkling to the east, across the channel, and on the opposite side of the tower there was just the suggestion of a pink glow in the sky, the last remnant of the dying day. Beneath that were a few more lights; probably Ellis River. He looked down, but there was nothing but blackness at his feet. Good. No sign of life on the island.

Just then he heard a distant sound; a throaty growl, rising and falling. A powerful engine, coming his way. A boat! He listened with mounting anxiety as the sound came closer, and closer, then died away to a deep purr as the engine was throttled down. Then it cut out altogether.

Diem waited in the darkness for what seemed an eternity. Then he heard voices and the sound of bushes breaking, and he looked down in time to see pin-points of light coming through the undergrowth. As they came closer he realised that they were torches, and as they swung from side to side he caught brief, half-illuminated glimpses of the figures of two men.

They disappeared from his view and Diem heard the sound of the door opening. Footsteps echoed around the empty chamber below. 'Move it, Pirelli!' a voice said. Diem cautiously sneaked down the stairs, just far enough to obtain a better view.

'There's too much moon for a job like this,' said the other voice.

'It'll be gone in a few hours,' said the first man impatiently. 'Give us some light.' There was the clatter and scrape of gear being moved about on the concrete floor, and then a sudden flare as a gas lamp was lit.

Diem crouched back into the shadows. He could see

them now. One, the man called Pirelli, was short and stocky, with a grotesque, over-large head, balding in front but with long, spiky wisps of hair protruding untidily from the back. His companion was tall, dark, and well-built, and as he turned in the gaslight Diem caught a glimpse of bushy eyebrows, a long, aquiline nose and flaring nostrils. Vo Diem sank further back. He was a survivor, able to sense danger instinctively, and he knew straight away that he was looking down at two tough customers.

Pirelli was crouched over something. Diem couldn't see what he was doing, but once or twice he heard the chink of glass on glass, and there was a clatter as a tool was dropped on the concrete. Pirelli cursed.

'Are you ready?' the tall man growled, standing over him. From his manner it was obvious that he was in charge.

'When I set this right, it'll start a neat little bonfire and leave no trace.' Pirelli replied. 'Just another household accident.' He stood up, holding something. The tall man bent to extinguish the lamp. A torch snapped on and Vo Diem heard the door open, then close. He sat on the hard steps in the sudden darkness listening as the soft crunching of their feet on the coral receded into the night and then they were gone. Diem was puzzled. These guys were up to no good; but what? He shrugged. It wasn't *his* problem. He made his way back upstairs much relieved to be once more on his own.

On Butterfly Island, the family were seated around the big table in the family-room, waiting as Mary served the food. It had been a long day and they were all hungry, but before anyone could begin to eat Charlie tapped his plate for attention. 'I've got something to say,' he announced.

'Come on, Charlie, the food's getting cold,' protested Andrew.

'This won't take long,' Charlie replied evenly. 'I just want to clear the air about this offer we got from David Lee. Seems like it's caused nothing but trouble.' At the mention of Lee's name a sudden quiet descended upon the room. Charlie felt all eyes upon him. 'When your mother died,' he continued, 'she left me two things in trust. One was you kids; the other was the love and care for this island. As far as *you're* concerned, I've tried to bring you up the way she'd have wanted.' He paused, and looked straight at Sally. 'I can't expect to hold on to you forever, but as far as Butterfly's concerned, it stays the way it is!' He coloured with emotion, and Sally felt a lump rising in her throat. Charlie went on: 'There'll be *no* David Lees, *no* millions of dollars. *Nothing* is going to shift me from this island.'

Suddenly he was acutely aware that he had nothing more to say. He stopped abruptly, his jaw quivering slightly with emotion. 'I just thought I ought to tell you how I feel,' he added awkwardly, his voice trailing off.

There was silence. Nobody moved. The lump in Sally's throat felt as big as a football now. At the opposite end of the table Andrew Wilson avoided his brother's eyes. Finally Charlie spoke again. 'Come on, eat up,' he said huskily. 'Your dinner's getting cold.'

Shortly after dinner, Charlie retired to the office, ostensibly to work, but he couldn't concentrate. He felt mentally and emotionally drained. Charlie was a man of action. He was at his best, *felt* at his best, when he was out in the open air, *doing* things. But this trouble with the business side of Butterfly was something else. You couldn't get to grips with it. It was real enough but not tangible; you couldn't *touch* it, not like a troublesome outboard motor or a leaking roof or a rotting jetty pile. It was a problem of the mind. He'd made his position very clear, but *that* wouldn't pay the bills. He looked at the clutter covering his desk. Paperwork. There was *always* paperwork to be done. He reached out and flicked half-heartedly through a stack of accounts, trying to sort them into some kind of priority, Gallio-Air's on top. There was no way they could pay them all right now. Charlie's stomach churned and he tossed them down again in dismay. He reached over and turned out the light.

He was still there at midnight, sitting in the darkness, thinking, brooding, long after everyone else had gone to bed. The moon had come up. It was hot, and still. Suddenly he became aware of another light; a dull, orange glow, reflected against the shiny foliage outside. Charlie stood up and crossed to the window and leaned out for a better view. His heart missed a beat. Towards the beach the palm trees were silhouetted stark and black against an angry glare. Something was on fire!

It was the workshop. The old building was well alight by the time Charlie arrived. Flames were roaring inside, licking out through the broken window and the numerous cracks and chinks in the walls. There were ominous creaks and groans as the corrugated iron roof, tortured by the heat, expanded and twisted, subjecting the ancient wooden frame to intolerable stresses and strains. Suddenly something let go. A sheet of iron peeled back with a sharp crack, and sparks rose like angry fireflies, glowing almost white, then bright orange, then dull red, before suddenly disappearing into the blackness of the night sky. Clouds of smoke billowed out, reflecting the glow of the inferno inside. Charlie tried to play an extinguisher through the window at the base of the flames but the heat drove him back.

Andrew ran up, clad only in pyjama trousers, extinguisher in hand, but the heat drove him back too. Behind them, a bell began to ring. Others arrived in pyjamas and nightdresses, breathless and scared. 'Greg, get the hose!' Charlie yelled. Another sheet of iron let go, releasing more sparks, and the flames roared up, reaching high into the sky. Some overhanging palms twisted and turned in the fiery blast, as if trying to turn and run away, but before long, they too, succumbed to the heat and burst into flames, the bushy tops flaring briefly before disappearing, leaving bare, blackened trunks to lean grotesquely into the fire's glow.

Greg came back with the hose but before they could use it there was a loud explosion, then another, and another. The flames had reached the cans of paint and solvent stored inside. Sheets of iron flew into the air, twisting end-over-end before landing dangerously close. The flames roared more fiercely than before. 'Get back!' yelled Charlie, shielding his face from the heat. At that moment he knew that there was nothing more they could do. The shed was doomed, and they were forced to stand and watch as the fire completed its work, greedily devouring everything that would burn.

Twenty minutes later it was all over. The workshop, built by Old Man Wilson all those years ago, was no more. Greg played the hose over the smouldering pile of ruins, the steam hissing as the water came into contact with the glowing embers and blackened corrugated iron. Mary came and stood close to Charlie. 'There's nothing you can do,' she said. She wanted to place a comforting hand on his shoulder, but stopped herself. Somehow, it wasn't the right thing to do.

'Get to bed!' Charlie snapped, staring at the smoking ruin. 'Get to bed, all of you.!' Mary turned and obeyed without another word. She understood. Shocked and grief-stricken, the others followed her lead; Sally and Jackie both crying, Greg ashen-faced.

But Andrew Wilson stayed. 'We helped Dad build this,' he said. 'It breaks my heart.'

'It breaks *your* heart!' Charlie bitterly echoed his words.

'Yeah. I'm sorry, Charlie,' said Andrew, genuinely upset.

'Why should *you* be sorry?' said Charlie savagely. 'You're half a breath away from getting what you want. I'm finished! I have no choice now. I *have* to sell Butterfly Island!'

EIGHT

Something heavy and hard dropped on to the concrete floor with a loud, hollow, metallic clang, jerking Vo Diem out of a restless sleep. He was on his feet instantly, ready to run even before he was properly awake. And then he realised where he was. He was still in the lighthouse, it was still dark, and the men were back!

'How long do we have to stay here?' It was Pirelli's voice.

'All night,' his companion replied gruffly. 'I should break your neck for bringing those tanks along!'

Tanks? Intrigued, Diem left his hiding-place and made his way silently back to his vantage point on the stairs. Down below, Pirelli was dragging something across the floor. 'They're worth a bit,' he puffed. 'It's a shame to see 'em wasted.' As he placed his burden against the wall and moved away, Diem leaned forward for a better look. Two metal cylinders: scuba diving tanks. Very interesting! Even more interesting was the neat design painted just below the valves: a swarm of yellow butterflies flying across an orange sun. The trademark of Butterfly Island, the same as on his life-jacket! Diem sat back on the steps, mystified. He was right. The men *had* been up to no good. But why steal two scuba diving tanks from Charlie Wilson in the middle of the night? It didn't add up.

'Suppose somebody spots the boat?' It was Pirelli again.

His colleague's reply was full of menace. 'Suppose *you* shift upstairs and see if you can spot that fire,' he snarled.

Diem's mind raced. What fire? Where? But there was no time for further thought. Pirelli was already on the stairs. Quickly, silently, Vo Diem moved ahead of him, climbing back up three steps at a time. He was in trouble now; trapped. There was no way out, except down, and the two men were between him and the door. He must hide. But where? He looked around desperately, listening with mounting panic to the measured beat of Pirelli's footsteps mounting the stairs. Just below the platform that support the mechanism for the light there was a narrow shelf leading in under the staircase. Diem wriggled into the confined space, taking his tell-tale life-jacket with him, shrank down to make himself as small as possible, and waited. The game was up. All Pirelli had to do was look down! It was a crazy place to hide, really, but it was the *only* place. He had no choice. Diem listened to the footsteps. Higher, higher, closer, closer! As Pirelli circled the spiral staircase the pool of light from his torch moved errily around the wall, its pale, probing fingers reaching further and further into Diem's refuge with every turn. Pirelli was very close now; almost upon him. Diem sank back into the meagre shadows, feeling vulnerable and exposed. He closed his eyes, waiting for the worst.

But nothing happened. The footsteps kept going, then a change in the sound told him that Pirelli was on the grating that ran around the top of the tower beside the light. Then there was silence. Diem opened his eyes. It was dark again. Pirelli had switched off his torch, but the beam from the light swept around with monotonous regularity, illuminating the platform and its surrounds. Diem peered up through the perforations of the metal mesh floor. Directly above, two dark silhouettes, side by side, broke up the regular diamond pattern. It took a few seconds for the shapes to take on any meaning, but then, suddenly, one moved, triggering off a spark of recognition in Diem's brain. His heart jumped. He was looking at the undersides of two shoes! Pirelli was standing right above him, his feet only centimetres away! Diem shrank back even further, watching as the shadows receded, stopped briefly on the other side of the tower, and then came back. Pirelli snapped on his torch again.

'Well?' His companion's voice came echoing up.

'It's out,' Pirelli replied, and began to clatter down the stairs. Diem breathed a sigh of relief, but he was puzzled. The fire had something to do with the Wilsons, because Pirelli had spent some time looking over towards Butterfly Island; and those were definitely the Wilson's tanks, probably stolen, down below. He couldn't see a connection, but one thing was certain; these were bad men. Diem thought about Jackie. She had been kind to him, and he hoped that she was all right. Quickly, almost by reflex, he shrugged the thought away. If the Wilsons were in trouble it wasn't *his* problem. He had to keep all his energies concentrated on his quest, and the immediate priority was to get off the island. These men had a boat; by the sound of its engine, a big one. It would be risky, but if he played his cards right, *that* was the way he would go!

As the grey dawn began to seep into his hiding-place, Diem made his move. The light had finished its work now, the mechanism had switched itself off for another day, and the early morning silence was broken only by the snores emanating from the two men, sprawled on their sleeping bags far below. Diem crept down the stairs, tip-toed past the two somnolent figures, and made his way to the door. It creaked slightly as he edged it open, but then he was through, running down towards the beach.

He knew where their boat would be: on the seaward side, making it invisible from Butterfly Island. A path through the undergrowth led him straight to it. He paused on the beach, more than pleased. He'd been right. It *was* big; at least ten metres overall, with a low profile that reeked of power and speed. A long foredeck curved up gracefully from the needle-sharp bow. There was an open cabin amidships, and then the after deck curved around a spacious cockpit, before dropping stylishly down again towards the steeply-raked transom. Diem grinned appreciatively: Charlie Wilson's old boat was a real bathtub compared with this lean, *mean* machine! He rubbed his hands in eager anticipation. What a way to go!

A small rubber dinghy was drawn up on the beach, but he ignored it, preferring instead to swim the few metres through the calm, warm water to where the cruiser was moored. A duckboard had been conveniently left down at the stern, and he used that to climb aboard. And then, a disappointment. There were no keys! Diem cursed himself for his oversight. He'd taken it for granted that the men would have left the ignition keys aboard. Ruefully he reminded himself that he wasn't dealing with the Wilsons now. He didn't relish the prospect of returning ashore and rummaging through the pockets of two potentially dangerous, sleeping men, but he could think of no alternative if he wanted to get away. Reluctantly Diem climbed back over the transom and was standing on the duckboard, ready to dive back into the water, when some sixth sense made him look towards the land. Instantly his blood ran cold. The men were on the beach! He scrambled back on board, landing in an undignified heap on the deck. Diem sneaked another cautious look. Pirelli was now pulling the rubber dinghy down the sand, while the other man watched him, hands idly in his pockets. Diem gritted his teeth; it was much too late to be thinking about picking trouser pockets now!

Keeping low, he made his way forward, acutely aware for the first time of the tracks that he had made earlier on the scrubbed deck planking with his dripping feet. They were drying quickly in the already-hot tropical sun, but he cursed himself for his carelessness: he'd been so *sure* about those damned keys that he'd ignored the most elementary precautions! But it was too late to be worrying about that now. He had to find a hiding-place, fast! He tried the cabin door. It was unlocked. Thankfully he slipped below and made his way through the luxuriously-appointed cabin, glancing around for some place, *any* place, where he could hide. There was a locker at the extreme bow, and he climbed over a bunk and hid himself in that, pulling the louvred door gently closed behind him. Then he held his breath, and waited.

He heard the men clumping about on deck; Pirelli grumbling as usual, and the other man's unmistakable, aggressive, tones ordering him about. But there were no shouts of discovery, no exclamations of alarm. Diem breathed a sigh of relief: they'd overlooked the foot-prints, by now thoroughly mixed up with their own. And then there was another voice, distorted and electronic. A two-way radio! Diem opened the locker door just a little so that he could hear better. 'We're on scramble,' the distorted voice said. 'Go ahead. Over.'

'The job's done. We're coming in. Over.' It was Pirelli's colleague: Diem could visualise him standing beside the set, microphone in hand.

'Stay where you are!' ordered the voice at the other end. 'Call back in two hours. Over.'

'Pirelli is getting a little nervous, Mr Lee. Over.'

The metallic voice exploded. 'You'll both do as you're told! I don't want either of you to show your faces until the accident investigation establishes that the fire was an accident! Over and out!'

There was a brief silence as the radio exchange ended, then a loud curse. Diem grinned. It was quite evident that Pirelli's mate didn't take kindly to being ordered about. Diem settled down and, for the first time in several hours, began to relax. Unlike the two men, he was quite content to wait. Slowly, so as not to attract attention, he closed the locker door.

On Butterfly Island, Charlie sat in the office, staring into space. Sally appeared at the door, a mug of coffee in hand. 'You haven't been to bed, have you?' she asked.

Charlie looked up. 'There's a lot of thinking to do,' he said absently.

'You always said it's crazy to make decisions when you're upset,' said Sally.

'Last night's fire wiped out our insurance cover,' replied Charlie sadly. 'I can't raise the capital to replace what was burnt.' He looked directly at her and she saw that his eyes were moist. 'We don't have a resort any more, Sal. We have to sell.'

'I didn't want it to happen like this, Dad,' she said.

Charlie forced a grin. 'At least the money we get can buy you kids a new start.' She left him then. She had to, or she would have burst into tears.

Outside, in the corridor, she met Mary, carrying a load of bed linen. 'Have you thought about what you're going to do?' she asked, following her into the family-room.

Mary set the basket down before she answered. 'To be honest, no,' she replied. 'I never believed it would come to this.'

'Neither did I,' said Sally gloomily. 'Not this way.'

Mary looked at her keenly. 'It's not *your* fault.'

'*Isn't* it? Dad wouldn't be giving up so easily, if I had backed him up.'

Mary shook her head. 'I wouldn't be seventeen again; not for all the tea in China!'

'Have you got anywhere to go?' Sally asked.

Mary laughed. 'I'll get by. Maybe your father will take another place on as manager. He's bound to need a housekeeper . . .'

'I could get a job, too,' interrupted Sally, suddenly enthusiastic, 'and Dad could always pick up work on the fishing boats . . .'

'What are you *talking* about? asked Mary, mystified by the change of mood.

Sally turned to face her. 'To keep the island, Dad has to make the mortgage payments, right?' As Mary nodded she went on excitedly, eyes ablaze. 'If we're *all* working, we might still do it! The Resort can stay closed until we think of some way to finance it!'

Mary looked at her in amazement. 'What ever happened to all those plans of yours about taking off to the big smoke?'

Sally shrugged. 'I want to do this first: not just for Dad. I guess I love this place more than I thought.'

Mary smiled. 'It's out of the question. There's no way we could afford it . . .' Her voice trailed off as she looked at Sally, full of enthusiasm, clutching desperately at straws, and she didn't have the heart to disillusion her. 'If your father goes for it,' she said at last, 'count me in.'

Sally's face lit up. 'He can't argue with the *whole family*!' she exclaimed, sweeping from the room. Mary was touched. It had taken a real crisis to make her do it, but for the first time *ever*, Sally had included her in the family circle instead of shutting her out. She bent to her work, sorting out the linen and folding it. She had loved her job on Butterfly with Charlie and the kids, and now, suddenly, it was all over! It was a real shame.

Suddenly aware of another presence, Mary looked up. Greg was standing glumly at the door. She forced a smile but he didn't respond; unusual for Greg, but understandable in the circumstances. 'Have you seen

Uncle Andrew?' he asked in a dull voice.

'He's gone over to Ellis River to see the solicitor, I think,' she replied. 'Have *you* seen young Jackie?'

'Nope,' replied Greg, still without expression. 'She's probably out feeding the lorikeets.' Another, gloomier thought occurred and his brow furrowed even more. 'Saying good-bye to 'em, more likely,' he added as he loped off.

At that moment lorikeets were the last thing on Jackie's mind. She was sitting in one of the Resort's outboard dinghies in the middle of the channel, concentrating hard on keeping straight in the short, steep chop that was tossing the tiny aluminium craft from side to side like a terrier shaking a rat. A big wave loomed up ahead. Jackie throttled back just in time. She felt the boat lift and hung on grimly as the bow went up, up, hung there for a moment, pointing at the sky, then dropped sickeningly, burying itself in a mass of green water and white spray. Jackie gritted her teeth. This was scary! But she was determined to put her theory about Vo Diem to the test. She *had* seen him that night, during the cyclone. And he *had* taken Greg's surf-ski. And there was only *one place* he could be: Beacon Island, dead ahead. She could see the lighthouse quite clearly now, white and clean above the trees.

Ten minutes later she was in calm water, sheltered by the land. She stopped the motor, gliding in until she felt the keel touch, then jumped out and dragged the dinghy up the beach as far as she could. She ran out the anchor and pushed it firmly into the coral sand with her foot, took off her life-jacket and tossed it into the boat, and made off towards the trees.

The lighthouse was deserted. She stood just inside the door, feeling very much alone. 'Diem-iem!' Her voice echoed off the walls as she called his name, but there was no reply. Her heart in her mouth, Jackie slowly climbed the spiral stairs. She called again, softly now, 'Diem, it's me . . . Jackie.' Still no reply. At the top she paused, her head protruding into the open space surrounding the light, but it was quite obvious that the gantry was deserted. Disappointed, she was turning to go down again when a bright splash of red and yellow under the stairs attracted her attention. She reached in and pulled out a life-jacket, and caught her breath when she saw that it was one of *theirs*! Yellow butterflies against an orange sun. Vo Diem *had been* here!

She ran down the steps two at a time, her head buzzing with possibilities. Maybe he was still on the island! He'd *have* to be! There was nowhere else for him to go! She'd find him if she had to comb the place from end to end! But suddenly at the bottom of the stairs she stopped dead in her tracks. In the doorway stood a man!

'Hello,' he said. He smiled with his mouth but his eyes were dull and cold. Jackie felt a shiver run up her spine. There was something menacing about the way he stood blocking the open door, his tall frame cutting out the light. 'What are you doing here?' the man asked, smiling again. Jackie didn't like the way his nostrils flared when he spoke.

'I'm here with a friend,' she replied. Better not to tell him that she was alone.

'Oh?' The man flicked his eyes up the stairs, then turned and glanced over his shoulder.

'He's not here now,' Jackie explained quickly.

'Oh?' said the man again. 'Where, then?'

'I don't know, exactly,' countered Jackie. This could easily get out of hand!

'What do you mean, you don't know?'

'He's hiding from me,' she said quickly. 'We're playing a game.'

'Well,' said the man, turning towards the door, 'let me help you track him down.' Jackie followed him outside, glad to be in the open air again. 'Maybe your friend is down there,' said the man, indicating a track that led off through the undergrowth towards the beach. Jackie was scared. She wanted to run in the opposite direction and get back into her dinghy and off the island *right now*. But she didn't. She started off down the track instead, the man following close behind. She knew she was taking a terrible risk but something inside her said that if she played along, he would take her to Vo Diem.

When they came out on to the beach she was surprised to see another man busily loading boxes into a rubber dinghy with the obvious intention of rowing them out to a big cruiser that was riding at anchor, close inshore. He stopped work and looked up at her, startled, as she approached. 'I'm afraid I gave this young lady quite a scare,' said the first man, still close behind. 'She's looking for a friend.'

'He's really good at hiding,' said Jackie, embellishing her story. 'Have you noticed food missing, or anything like that?'

The man at the rubber boat stared back, then shook his head. 'We've only been here an hour or so,' he said gruffly, then glanced at his companion. 'We'd better shove off, Madden, if we want to get some fish.' Then she noticed two air tanks, lying on the sand. They were decorated with yellow butterflies against an orange sun. Suddenly everything became crystal clear and it was too much for her to handle. She panicked, turned, and *ran*.

Why she made for the lighthouse she never knew. She was well aware that it was a dead end, that she was trapped, even as she was pounding up the stairs, the footsteps of her pursuers echoing behind her. At the top she ran on to the parapet and looked down over the side. Too far to jump. She moved back to the head of the stairs, panting like a hunted animal. The life-jacket lay where she'd left it. She picked it up, fumbled frantically in her pocket and produced a stub of marker crayon, and began to write.

She didn't have much time, but she managed to scribble down all that she wanted to say and toss the jacket back under the stairs before the man named Madden loomed up, hot and bothered and out of breath. 'Well, well,' he breathed. He wasn't smiling now.

'What are we gonna do?' panted his companion, coming up behind.

Madden's eyes narrowed. 'She knows,' he said. 'Don't ask me how, but she *knows*!' and with that he lunged forward and seized Jackie by the wrists and half-carried, half-pulled her, struggling, down the stairs.

Back on Butterfly, Charlie looked up from his paperwork to see Mary standing at the office door. 'Jackie's missing,' was all she said, but it was enough to tell him that something was drastically wrong. Mary was not one to make a song-and-dance over nothing.

'There's a boat gone, Dad,' said a worried-looking Greg.

Charlie stood up, paperwork and financial worries instantly dispelled from his mind. 'She knows she's not to go out alone without telling someone,' he said. He went over to the radio and picked up the microphone. It took only a few seconds to establish contact with Bob, in the air on a tourist run. 'Jackie's somewhere out on the reef in one of our outboards, Bob. Can you keep an eye out for her? Over.'

The reply came crackling back. 'Well, I've got a few *errands* to run, Mr Wilson.' Bob paused, allowing the sarcasm to sink in. 'But no problems; I'll keep my eyes open. Over and out.'

Charlie smiled grimly as he replaced the mike on its cradle. 'No problems,' he said. 'That's *easy* to say when you're twenty-one.'

'Dad,' said Greg hesitantly, 'I think she's gone out looking for Vo Diem.'

Charlie winced. 'Oh, no! Not that again!'

'She's been real spooked since the cyclone,' said Greg. 'She really believes she saw him at the window that night.'

Charlie wasn't entirely convinced. 'Did she actually *say* anything to you about going out after him?' he asked.

'No . . .' Greg began, but he was interrupted by Bob's callsign, blaring from the radio. All eyes flashed to the speaker as they listened to the electronic, distorted voice. 'I'm over Beacon Island, Mr Wilson,' said Bob 'and there's an outboard on the beach. Over.'

Charlie grapped the mike. 'Any sign of Jackie? Over.'

'Negative. Just the boat. Over and out.'

Charlie turned to Greg. 'Come on son, let's go and bring her back!'

It took them the best part of an hour to get over to Beacon Island, but half-way across the channel, through the glasses, Greg spotted the outboard, drawn up on the beach. Charlie anchored *Elizabeth* in deep water to allow for the ebbing tide, then sounded the hooter loud and long, expecting at any moment to see Jackie's tiny figure emerge from the bush and stand, waving, on the beach. But she didn't appear. Concern mounting, he and Greg lowered a dinghy and went ashore. The empty aluminium boat was well up on the sand. Charlie reached down and picked up Jackie's life-jacket, lying on the deck. 'Little monkey!' he muttered to himself, very worried now.

They separated then and moved inland, combing the bush and calling her name, but there was no human response, just the screeching of disturbed sea birds wheeling above them in the clear, pale blue sky. At the lighthouse they met up again, empty handed. Charlie was puzzled by the open door; the tower was usually kept locked. 'Jackie!' he called softly. No reply.

Inside, they made their way up the stairs. At the top Charlie used the height to advantage and made a slow, careful check of the whole island. He looked back towards Butterfly, then at *Elizabeth*, then at their dinghy, drawn up beside Jackie's boat on the sand. He crossed to the other side of the tower and made a careful inspection of the seaward side. The beach there was empty, too.

'Dad!' Greg was standing at the top of the stairs, a life-jacket in his hand. At first Charlie thought it was Jackie's, but then he remembered that they had left that in the boat on the beach. 'I found it *there*,' said Greg, indicating the shelf under the stairs. Charlie took the jacket and turned it over in his hands. And then he saw the message: three words, scrawled in crayon on the yellow plastic, in a large, childish hand:

FIRE WAS SET.

As soon as he and Greg returned to Butterfly Island, Charlie called a council-of-war. Standing in the centre of the family-room he gave everyone a quick run-down on events so far, and then followed up with the possibilities. He was acutely aware of just how little they really knew. It was mainly guesswork; a lot of 'ifs', 'buts' and 'maybes'; extremely frustrating but in the absence of any definite leads the best they could do. 'If Jackie *was* on that island, we'd have *found* her!' he declared, brandishing the life-jacket that they had discovered on the stairs.

'Well, *somebody* wrote that message,' said Andrew.

'And it was probably Jackie,' added Greg.

'But it's not *her* life-jacket!' Charlie declared. 'Her's was still in the outboard!'

Greg wouldn't buy that argument entirely. 'She still could have written the message on it,' he pointed out.

'Maybe she ran out of fuel,' suggested Andrew. 'Did you check?' Charlie shook his head; he hadn't.

'*I* did,' said Greg. 'She had plenty.'

'Then she left that island with somebody else,' declared Charlie. 'And that somebody wants. . . .' He couldn't bring himself to say more; the very thought of anyone harming Jackie made his blood turn cold. He whirled on Sally, standing by the radio. 'Sal, I want you to start calling around,' he ordered brusquely. 'Make up a roster. I want somebody at that radio right around the clock! I'm going back on the water!' Mary watched as he headed determinedly for the door; Charlie was at his best when there were things to be done. She followed him outside.

'Charlie,' she called. He stopped, turned and faced her, anxious to be on his way. 'There could be any number of explanations,' she said, forcing a reassuring smile.

He nodded, 'Maybe,' he said, 'but you can't help thinking about the first one that comes to mind.'

Jackie sat on a bunk in the forward cabin of the big cruiser, dazed, shocked, her mind in a whirl. Here she was, a prisoner, for the second time in a week! It couldn't *really* be happening! It had to be a dream; one of those bad ones that recur, over and over again. But, deep inside, she knew that it wasn't. The stark reality of her situation slammed home and she shivered with fear. She'd been scared when Vo Diem had taken *Elizabeth*; really scared; but this was different. She was close to panic now. Madden had hurt her, back in the lighthouse. She rubbed her wrists, bruised as she had struggled against his vice-like grip. He was very strong, but she had managed to get in a few kicks as he dragged her down the stairs. He'd have sore shins to remember her by, and that knowledge cheered her up.

The roar of the powerful engines suddenly subsided,

and she leaned forward to peer through the tiny port-hole that was her only window on the outside world. The boat was heading up a creek. The water had taken on a dirty brown colour, and mangroves were sliding past quite close, their twisted roots and gnarled trunks rising at crazy angles from the muddy bank. As she watched, the cruiser slowed further, the engines burbling noisily now at idling speed. The bank came closer and closer.

Then Jackie heard the sound of a key in the lock and she turned from the porthole to see Pirelli standing at the cabin door. 'Come on,' he growled, jerking a thumb towards the cockpit. Without a word she climbed off the bunk and made her way up on deck, noting with some satisfaction that he gave her a wide berth as she went past.

She had a better view from the cockpit, and she was able to get her bearings. They were obviously on the mainland now, some distance from the sea. The creek was very narrow, surrounded on all sides by swamp. Mangroves reached over the cruiser, branches meeting overhead in a tangled, vivid green canopy, cutting out the light. A few shafts of sunlight managed to struggle through, illuminating pools of dirty water and broad expanses of evil-looking mud, spiked everywhere by needle-sharp mangrove roots, poking through. The whole gloomy scene reminded Jackie of a horror movie she had once seen at the Ellis River Drive-In; a girl had been lost in this enchanted forest and. . . .

Madden cut the engines, bringing her back to the here and now. The cruiser was gliding towards a ramshackle jetty, and beyond that a dilapidated shack was just visible through trees. The air was very hot, very steamy, and very still. The only sounds were the gurgling of the wake and the faint, high-pitched screaming of thousands of mosquitoes, which began to descend upon them in waves.

The men made her lead the way up the muddy path to the shack, which was set about half-a-metre above the mud, on wooden piles, out of reach of high tides. The place was in appalling condition. The corrugated iron walls and roof were rusty and pitted with holes. The windows gaped open like mouths with jagged, discoloured, transparent teeth. There was no door, just a couple of badly corroded hinges, hanging at crazy angles. Jackie stopped. She didn't want to go inside; being in the open air gave her the illusion of being free, even if she was not. Pirelli stepped forward, grabbed her shoulders and propelled her through the door. Madden followed them inside, then tossed a hank of rope to Pirelli. 'Tie her up,' he ordered.

'Aw, come on!' Pirelli protested.

'Tie her up!' insisted Madden. 'In there; hands and feet.' He indicated the adjoining room.

Pirelli still hesitated. Jackie tried to pull away but he held her fast. 'My Dad's going to come after me!' she yelled, struggling and kicking as hard as she could. 'He'll have every policeman on the coast with him, too!'

'The kid's right,' said Pirelli. 'Listen, Madden, we could cut our losses and . . .'

'Tie her up,' said Madden again. 'She knows my *name*. She knows who I *am*, thanks to you!'

A few minutes later Jackie was lying on the hard floor, securely bound. Pirelli wasn't taking any chances; he had tied her tightly, and the ropes bit into her ankles and wrists. She wriggled about, trying to minimise the discomfort and after a while the sharpness of the pain changed to a dull, numbing ache, like pins and needles. She guessed that the tightness of her bonds was cutting off her circulation. But it wasn't the ropes that caused her the most distress; it was the mosquitoes. While her hands were free she could at least slap and scratch, but now she was utterly helpless and unable to do a thing to stop them as they landed on her in hundreds, biting painfully every square centimetre of exposed skin.

A plane flew overhead. 'You reckon they're looking for her?' Pirelli asked anxiously.

'Maybe,' said Madden.

'We wouldn't be in this spot if we'd got off Beacon Island!' complained Pirelli.

'It was Lee's idea that we stayed,' Madden replied evenly.

'It's not *him* in the hot seat,' Pirelli moaned. '*We're* the ones who kidnapped her!'

Madden looked down at Jackie, and the gleam in his eye made her blood run cold. 'This job just became very expensive,' he said.

They left the shack then, but a few minutes later Pirelli returned, carrying sleeping bags, the transistor radio, and a box of supplies. He switched on the radio and busied himself preparing a simple meal to a background of country music. As Jackie listened she felt despair welling up inside her. She had heard those familiar sounds of the Ellis River radio station hundreds of times, at home, and right now Butterfly Island and her Dad and Sally and Greg and Mary seemed a million miles away! She wondered if she would ever see them again.

Pirelli came over to her, carrying a plastic plate. He knelt beside her, set it down on the floor, and untied her hands. 'Now don't you give me any trouble,' he warned, standing up and moving away. Jackie didn't bother to reply. She sat up and rubbed her hands together, wincing with pain as the circulation returned, then picked up the plate. It was ages since she had eaten, but her appetite had deserted her, and she merely picked at her food.

Madden appeared at the door. 'I've just been on the blower to Lee,' he announced. 'We wait here overnight and radio in again at ten o'clock tomorrow morning.'

'Radio in at ten *tomorrow* morning!' repeated Pirelli.

'What's he playing at? We're sitting ducks! If they search this area. . . .'

'He's scared to death,' interrupted Madden. 'Like you.'

Jackie piped up. 'I bet you wrecked our canoes and bashed Greg,' she said accusingly, wondering where she was finding the courage to speak at all. 'You probably did *all* the things we blamed on Diem! I bet you were the ones setting off explosions on the reef, too.'

Madden came and stood over her. She cringed, expecting the worst, but he merely knelt beside her and snatched away the plate of food. 'You're not really hungry, kid,' he said. 'When you *are* you'll shut up.' He stood up and glared at Pirelli. 'Tie her hands!' he ordered. 'If she opens her mouth again, gag her!'

Pirelli moved in to obey. 'You reckon we can trust Lee?' he asked, deftly applying the rope to Jackie's wrists.

'Sure,' said Madden.

'Suppose he decides to do a deal with the cops?'

'He's in too deep,' said Madden.

Pirelli finished the job. 'I don't like it,' he said, standing up. 'I don't like this at all. If we'd left the lighthouse when I said, we'd be well away from here by now!'

'Shut up!' snapped Madden. 'You take your orders from *me*! Do as you're told and you'll be all right.'

'Oh yeah?' returned Pirelli sceptically. 'I don't know if I can trust you any more than I can trust Lee.'

Madden shrugged. 'That's a chance you've got to take!' He studied his colleague's face carefully for several seconds before going on. 'We're going to do a deal with Mr Lee,' he said evenly.

'What kind of deal?' asked Pirelli, not really interested.

Madden dropped his voice. 'I'm going to get back on the radio,' he said, 'I'm going to tell Lee that we want

153

two bank accounts opened at his bank in Brisbane, in our names, fifty grand in each.'

Pirelli's eyes popped. 'That's *extortion*!' he gasped.

Madden indicated Jackie, lying on the floor. '*That's* kidnapping,' he said.

Pirelli began to pace agitatedly about the room, quite obviously out of his league. 'We're not worth a *hundred thousand bucks* to David Lee!' he said.

Madden smiled. 'Oh, no?' he asked. 'Think about it, Pirelli. There are only three people who can put him away for a long time; you, me, and the kid. For fifty grand I'm sure you'd be willing to disappear *real* fast.'

Pirelli nodded, then a thought occurred to him. 'What about the kid?'

Madden didn't even look at Jackie. 'Once the money's in the bank,' he said, 'she disappears too. For good.'

NINE

Charlie was almost beside himself with worry. He had spent hours on the water, visiting neighbouring islands, combing every inlet, closely examining every stretch of deserted beach, sounding *Elizabeth's* hooter until his ears were ringing, but of Jackie there was no sign. Finally, at four o'clock, as tense as a watch spring, he called Pat Connolly on the two-way and asked for help. It was time to bring in the professionals now.

The Sergeant lost no time in coming over from Ellis River, but nevertheless the shadows were lengthening as the whole family met him on the Butterfly Island jetty.

'I've checked with the doctors, Pat, and the hospitals,' Charlie began, but Andrew Wilson interrupted.

'Let's not get hysterical, Charlie,' he said. 'There's probably a simple, logical explanation.'

'*Hysterical*!' Charlie exploded. 'She's been missing for *eight hours*! What would you like me to do? Put an ad in the paper?'

Connolly saved the situation. 'I've been thinking about the boy, Vo Diem,' he said calmly. 'Jackie thought he was still alive.' He looked questioningly at Charlie. 'You said on the radio that there was an extra life-jacket at the lighthouse?' Charlie nodded. 'Then maybe she was *right*,' the policeman said. 'She could be trying to help the lad escape, like she did before.'

'Where does *that* get us?' Charlie asked.

'It could stop our imaginations going off half-cocked, for a start,' returned Connolly evenly.

'So, what do we do now?'

'We keep looking,' the policeman said.

They dispersed then, and searched for Jackie without success until dark, when Connolly returned to Ellis River, promising that they'd begin again, on a larger scale, at first light. His last words to Charlie were, 'We'll find her, mate. Don't worry,' but beneath his calm exterior, he was very concerned.

Jackie spent a terrible night. Pirelli freed her hands and she was able to eat a little, but he tied her up again as soon as she had finished, and she stayed that way for the rest of the night, tossing restlessly on the hard floor, her limbs growing increasingly numb. The mosquitoes almost drove her to distraction, biting and buzzing ceaselessly around her head. Slaps and curses from the next room gave her some consolation: at least they were annoying her captors, too. Finally she managed to drift off into an uneasy sleep.

In the early hours she had a horrible dream. There was a huge mosquito under the hut. She could hear it moving about, and then she felt it boring its way up through the floorboards, and into her back. It was *hurting*! She yelped and rolled away. In a cold, fearful sweat, she made herself look back, expecting to see a monstrous proboscis rising through the floor, followed by a loathsome head. But instead, all she saw was a piece of stiff straw, protruding through a crack in the floorboards and moving about and suddenly she realised that she was awake, and it was light, and somebody underneath the floor had been poking at her with the straw to gain her attention. And then she heard a low voice. 'Jackie, Jackie . . .'

'What? Who is that?' she whispered fearfully.

'It's me. Diem.'

Her heart leapt. 'What are *you* doing here?'

'What do you *think*?' said the voice from underneath the floorboards. 'I'm going to bust you *out* of there.'

Suddenly she remembered the men. 'Shh!' she whispered urgently.

'It's OK,' came the reply. 'They're on the boat.' Jackie wriggled around painfully so that she could see into the next room. It was empty.

'Roll out of the way,' ordered Diem. Jackie was puzzled, but this was not the time to be asking questions, so she obeyed. She felt a series of shocks, then the sound of splitting timber, and suddenly a blue and white sneaker came bursting through the rotten floorboards. She understood now: Vo Diem was underneath the building, on his back, kicking his way through the floor. Jackie's heart leapt again. Some mosquito! The shocks continued, bits and pieces of timber flying everywhere under the onslaught of Diem's pounding feet. Finally he had made a sizeable hole. His head appeared.

'Quick! Untie me!' whispered Jackie. Diem hoisted himself up, sat on the edge, and to her surprise, suddenly began to suck his finger. 'What's wrong?' she asked urgently.

'Splinter,' he replied.

'Oh, for heaven's *sake*!' she exclaimed, wriggling around so that he could get at her wrists. The knots were small and tight, and it seemed an eternity before he had her hands free. They throbbed painfully as the renewed blood supply surged through the arteries and veins. In another minute her feet were untied, too, and Diem was helping her as she lowered herself through the hole.

They crouched together under the building, and looked anxiously towards the creek. There was no sign of the men. 'This way,' said Vo Diem, and then he was gone, doubling across an open space to the cover of a clump of mangroves. Jackie tried to follow, but her legs refused to move properly and she fell, face down, in the mud. He came back.

'I'm all stiff!' she wailed. Diem glanced towards the creek but made no move to help her to her feet. 'I can't walk!' moaned Jackie, tears streaming down her mud-splattered face, but she wasn't about to get any sympathy from Vo Diem. 'Try *running*,' he said, and then he was gone, sprinting off through the trees. Jackie's heart sank. Surely he wouldn't desert her! Then she realised that there was little more that he could do. He couldn't *carry* her; she was too big. It was up to her now; a case of sink or swim. Painfully she hauled herself on to her feet.

Vo Diem was waiting for her behind some trees, and as she lurched towards him he ran off again, setting a cracking pace through the swamp. They made noisy progress, splashing through shallow pools of brown water and squelching through the mud. There were razor-sharp mangrove roots everywhere; one false step would mean disaster. Jackie didn't allow herself even to think about crocodiles; Pirelli and Madden were bad enough!

Try as she might, after a few minutes she was exhausted. Grabbing a mangrove branch to prevent herself from falling, she called out to Diem: 'I can't keep running like this!' He stopped some metres ahead, then turned and came back.

'You move fast; then they can't shoot you,' he said. For a moment Jackie thought that he was joking, but one look at his face told her that he wasn't. Again her heart missed a beat. '*Shoot* me?' she said.

Diem ignored the question. 'Listen, I want to make a deal.'

'*What*?'. Jackie was staggered by the suggestion, but he was dead serious.

'Back at that place, Ellis River, there is a fishing boat. I heard about it on the radio. It's going to Indonesia.'

His eyes bored into hers. 'If I get you out of here, you help *me* get on that boat.'

'What?' said Jackie, incredulously, again.

'Is it a *deal*?' he pressed.

Jackie shrugged. 'It's a deal,' she said.

'OK!' said Vo Diem, slapping her on the hand in the way he'd learned from the Americans, back home in Vietnam. Then he took her by the arm and led the way off through the swamp.

They hadn't gone far when he stopped suddenly and listened, tense and alert. 'What . . .' Jackie began, but he pressed a finger to his lips, silencing her. She listened too. Behind them, not far away, was the sound of breaking twigs and wading feet. 'They're after us!' said Jackie despairingly. Vo Diem quickly looked around, then half-led, half-dragged her to the base of a big mangrove tree.

'Up there! Quick!' he said, hoisting her up. It was an easy climb, because the tree was growing out of the mud at a shallow angle, like a ramp, and there were plenty of hand-holds on the knobbly trunk. When she reached a fork several metres above the ground Jackie paused and looked down. The ground was almost completely hidden by leaves. Good. This was far enough; as long as they kept still they'd be invisible here. She wriggled over to make room for Vo Diem.

No sooner had he settled in beside her than Madden and Pirelli were below them. Peering down through the foliage, Jackie caught a glimpse of Madden, soaked to the skin, in the lead, sloshing through the mud at a furious pace. Pirelli, whose legs were shorter, was just behind, even wetter still, and floundering along in his colleague's wake.

When all sounds of their progress had gone, Diem led the way down from the tree. Jackie followed and in her haste, slipped and fell. It was only a matter of a metre or so, into soft mud, but it was enough. A sharp pain stabbed up her right leg. She screamed. Diem went white. The men would have heard that! 'Get up!' he hissed.

Jackie tried but couldn't. 'My ankle!' she said. Diem reached down and pulled her roughly to her feet. She tried to walk, stumbled, fell, and got up again. She stayed up this time, hobbling along, but she was very slow; too slow for Vo Diem. He took his hand away.

'You can't make it. Sorry,' he said.

Jackie's eyes widened in horror. 'Diem! Don't leave me!' she begged, but he backed away, then turned, and was gone. With a horrible sinking feeling Jackie listened to the sound of his fleeing footsteps. And then she heard something else and her heart rose into her mouth; more footsteps. Pirelli and Madden; coming back!

She offered no resistance as Pirelli picked her up and carried her bodily back to the hut where once again she was bound and, at Madden's insistence, gagged. Surprisingly, they didn't ask how she had managed to get away, but from Madden's attitude it was obvious that he thought Pirelli's knots had been to blame. Quailing under his leader's sharp tongue, Pirelli was taking no chances this second time, tying double knots, extra tight, and it wasn't long before she felt the now-familiar numbness as her circulation was cut off once again. Jackie was close to breaking point now; freedom had never seemed so far away! Tears welled up in her eyes, overflowed, and trickled down both cheeks.

Madden walked towards the door. 'I'm going to Ellis River,' he announced.

Pirelli looked up from the radio. 'What for?' he asked.

'One of us has to get to a phone, stupid!' said Madden.

Pirelli still didn't understand.

'We have to make sure Lee's keeping his part of the bargain,' explained Madden, as if he were speaking to a three-year-old. 'We have to be sure that the money's *there*.'

'How do I know you're going to come back?'

'Because if the money's there, then things will have to be done here,' replied Madden, looking down at Jackie, 'and you haven't got the stomach for it.' Her skin prickled. She knew exactly what he meant.

When Madden backed the cruiser out of the creek and headed up the coast towards Ellis River, Vo Diem was once again comfortably ensconced in his hiding-place in the bow. He was sorry that he had abandoned Jackie, but she had left him no choice. Where he came from, only the fittest survived.

It wasn't far to Ellis River, and Diem stayed in hiding, listening to the engines slow, then stop. He heard Madden moving about, and then all sounds of activity aboard ceased. Carefully, Diem opened the locker door and stepped down into the cabin. He made his way to a porthole and looked out. He watched as Madden left the marina and stepped into a public telephone outside some shops. Quickly Diem crossed the cabin and looked through the porthole on the other side.

There she was! The unmistakable lines of an Indonesian fishing vessel, tied up on the opposite side of the channel. The *Sea Tiger*! All he had to do now was get aboard. But a shock awaited him. Madden had locked the cabin door! Disappointed, Diem rattled it, shook it, then put his shoulder to it and heaved with all his might, but it refused to budge. He gave it a desperate, savage blow, but succeeded only in almost breaking his hand. Grimacing with pain, he glanced through the porthole. Another shock: Madden was on his way back. It was too late to get away undiscovered now. With mounting dismay he listened to the engines start again, then watched as the *Sea Tiger* slid away past the port-hole and disappeared astern. So near and yet so far!

Jackie was making the most of Madden's absence.

When Pirelli had offered her a drink she had nodded her head vigorously, and he had taken off the gag. She drank deeply from the cup that he held up to her lips, then turned her head away. He paused, allowing her to rest. 'Can't you untie my hands?' she asked, putting on her most appealing voice.

'No way!' said Pirelli emphatically, adding, almost by way of apology: 'It's your own fault.'

Jackie sensed his guilt. 'Suppose Mr Madden doesn't come back?' she asked innocently.

'He'll be back.'

'But suppose he doesn't?' she pressed, working on his insecurity.

'Give it a miss,' grumbled Pirelli. He reached across to re-apply the gag.

'You could let me *go*,' pleaded Jackie, turning her head away.

'Very funny!' he said.

'I bet they'd let you off,' she went on quickly. 'I could tell them Mr Madden had a gun, and he *made* you help him.'

Pirelli paused, looking at her hard, and Jackie felt her spirits soaring. She had him rattled now; he was fighting with himself. She was almost there! But then he grabbed her head. 'Madden will be back,' Pirelli said, stuffing the cloth into her mouth. Jackie felt sick. That was probably her last chance.

Madden did return. 'Two hours, you said!' grumbled Pirelli. 'Where the hell have you been?' Madden ignored him. 'Is the money there?' Pirelli asked.

Madden smiled; a slow, contemptuous leer. 'It's there,' he said. 'Fifty grand each. Get ready to move out. We take the kid with us.' Pirelli scuttled about, loading their supplies back on board, and removing all traces of their occupancy of the shack. When finally he came back for the last time and picked Jackie up she offered no resistance; her spirits were very low.

Once aboard, she was untied, and locked in the cabin. She lay on a bunk, rubbing her numb limbs back into life and by the time they reached the mouth of the creek her circulation had begun to return and with it, sensation. She could feel her toes and fingertips again. Her arms and legs were stiff and sore, and her ankle was throbbing, but at least she could move around.

Jackie looked out through the porthole. Spray was flashing past, smudging the glass, and by the movement of the deck and the roar of the engines, she estimated that they were back at full speed, heading for the open sea. But where exactly were they going? What was going to happen to her when they arrived? She remembered the look on Madden's face and his words, back in the shack. 'She disappears too; for good.' She shuddered. Where was her Dad now? Surely he was still out looking for her? Surely he hadn't given up hope?

Pirelli appeared at the door, bracing himself against the pitching of the deck. 'Come on. Madden wants you,' he called above the engines' roar, and as Jackie climbed down off the bunk to obey she felt the big cruiser begin to slow down.

She stood in the cockpit between her captors and looked back along the wake. The mainland mountains were indistinct patches of smoky blue, low down on the horizon, indicating that the cruiser was a long way out to sea; much further than she'd been with Vo Diem. The sun was high; about eleven o'clock. Craning her neck and standing on tip-toe, Jackie peered forward over the cockpit coaming. A small cay lay about a hundred metres ahead. It was obviously their destination, because as she watched, Madden slowed the big vessel further, guiding it over the shallows towards the low expanse of sand. ·

As they grounded gently he turned to Pirelli. 'Put her ashore,' he ordered matter-of-factly.

'I don't get it,' said Pirelli, scratching his head.

'Tide's on the way in, running fast,' explained Madden. 'Another hour, and this cay will be six feet under water. So will anything left on it.'

Instinctively Jackie gripped the polished handrail that ran around the edge of the cockpit. 'No!' she yelled.

Pirelli lumbered towards her. 'Come on,' he said. He grabbed her roughly, but she held on tightly, kicking him in the shins as he prised her fingers free, picked her up bodily, and tossed her over his shoulder in a fire-man's grip. Jackie knew she was fighting for her life now. She wriggled and squirmed and clawed and scratched and kicked, grabbing anything and everything within reach. She knew she could not win: she was merely delaying the inevitable. Pirelli was a strong man and she was just a twelve-year-old, but at least she was going down fighting.

Finally they reached the bow. Pirelli lifted her up and tried to push her over the side but she clung to the pulpit, wrapping arms and legs around the rail and hanging on like a leech.

'Hurry up! Ditch her!' she heard Madden call. Pirelli cursed then jumped down on to the sand and reached up and grabbed from below. He could bring his entire weight to bear now, and she was forced to let go, but the sudden release upset Pirelli's balance and when he fell she went with him, one arm wrapped tightly around his neck, the other pounding out a furious tattoo on the small of his back. As Pirelli struggled to free himself of his fighting, kicking, clawing, burden, Madden left the controls and made his way to the bow. 'Come on man!' he yelled impatiently.

Suddenly there was a roar and the boat surged backwards. Madden, leaning over the pulpit rail, found himself describing a neat somersault through the air. He landed ingloriously (and painfully) on his stomach, and came up spitting sand and salt water to see the cruiser moving rapidly backwards away from the shore.

Through stinging, sand-choked eyelids he caught a glimpse of a small, dark figure at the controls.

'Diem!' Jackie shrieked. She let go of Pirelli and began to struggle through the shallows towards the boat.

'Grab her!' yelled Madden, but Pirelli just stood and gaped: events were moving far too quickly for him. Cursing, Madden began to run. He overtook Jackie in a few strides and scooped her up.

'Go and get help, Diem! Get help!' she cried, hammering away ineffectually at Madden's back. Safely out of reach now, Diem slammed the power levers into neutral. The boat slowed, the engines burbling noisily, awaiting his command.

'You come back here, boy!' Madden roared, but Diem ignored him. With one quick, final glance at Jackie he pushed the levers all the way forward and the cruiser responded instantly, leaping out of the water like a greyhound off its leash, accelerating away from the cay with a thunderous roar.

Madden put Jackie down, and all three stood on the sand, shading their eyes and watching the boat as it rapidly disappeared towards the west. A wave broke over Madden's feet. 'That kid; he'll come back for you?' he asked her anxiously. 'He wouldn't *leave* you here?'

'I don't know,' said Jackie truthfully. 'I don't know *what* he'll do, now that he's got your boat.'

Another wave broke, slightly higher than the first.

On Butterfly Island, Andrew Wilson was sitting in the office, talking to Sergeant Connolly on the two-way radio as Charlie and Greg came into the room. 'Check my facts out, Sergeant,' he said. 'I think they give the man sufficient motive. Over.'

Connolly's voice came back. 'If you're right, you've set the cat among the pigeons this time, Andrew. Over and out.'

'What was all *that* about?' Charlie asked.

'Take over the radio, Greg,' Andrew said. He threw his brother a sobre glance, indicating that they should talk outside, and Charlie followed him into Reception. Andrew paused, choosing his words carefully before he spoke. 'I've just received information about David Lee, which I've passed on to Connolly,' he said, serious-faced. 'He might be responsible for Jackie's disappearance.'

Charlie's jaw dropped. 'What? David Lee?'

Andrew nodded. 'That message, scrawled on the life-jacket: "Fire was set". If Jackie *did* write it, she must have meant the fire at the workshop. Someone deliberately set the fire, and Jackie found out while she was at the lighthouse.'

'OK,' said Charlie. 'But what's that got to do with David Lee?'

'He's nearly broke, Charlie,' replied Andrew. 'His companies are beginning to collapse like dominoes, and his creditors are moving in. Butterfly Island was going to bail him out.'

Charlie gave a short, mirthless laugh. 'That's ridiculous!'

Andrew shook his head. 'Lee got hold of a confidential Government survey.' He leaned forward dramatically: 'Charlie, Butterfly's sitting on top of a lake of *oil*!'

Charlie was staggered now. '*Oil*?' he gasped, and then: 'How come *you* know so much about this?'

Andrew gulped. 'Lee offered me fifty thousand dollars to influence you to sell. That made me suspicious, so I played along until I could find out what he was up to . . .'

Charlie cut his confession short. 'You miserable. . . .' Words failed him then for a moment, and his jaw hardened before he went on. 'The workshop was burnt, canoes were smashed, there was that explosion out on

166

the reef, they were testing for the oil, of course!' It all added up now. He turned on his brother, white with anger, fists clenched. 'And now they've got Jackie,' he growled accusingly, 'And *you knew* what was going on!'

'I never connected Lee with all that till just now, when I learned about the oil,' protested Andrew. 'It's worth a lot more than a million dollars!'

That was the final straw. Charlie lashed out, releasing all his anger in one tremendous blow which landed fair and square on his brother's jaw. Andrew staggered back against the counter, eyes rolling and knees sagging, and went down.

Charlie stood over him. 'You can talk *money* when my *daughter's* out there?' he snarled.

'Charlie,' said Andrew groggily from the floor, 'for the record, I *had* to give Lee enough rope to hang himself, but the only thing I give a *damn* about is Jackie!'

Charlie snorted with contempt. 'Then you'd better hope and pray that we find her,' he said, turned on his heel and left the room.

The cruiser had settled into her stride now, the long nose lifting and dipping, lifting and dipping easily over the translucent, blue-green swells. Vo Diem was feeling good. He had a powerful boat all to himself, and at long last, he was free! There'd be no running around on the coral this time: he'd learnt *that* lesson. He fed the wheel slowly from hand to hand, watching with satisfaction as the compass moved gently in response. He was heading towards Indonesia, travelling north, *inside* the reef!

But as the minutes ticked by, taking him further and further away from the cay, and Jackie, he began to have doubts. No matter how hard he tried, he couldn't dismiss her from his mind. Once more he saw that pitiful, frightened, face. Again he heard her desperate words ringing in his ears: *Go and get help, Diem! Get help!* He thought of Charlie Wilson, no doubt looking in the wrong place. By the time the search was widened to include the cay it would be too late: Jackie would no longer be there. His eye was drawn to the two-way radio, its spiral-wound microphone cord gently swaying to the movement of the boat, and an idea began to form. Charlie must be *told*! It was the *least* he could do!

He flicked on the radio, then hesitated. It would mean the end of his quest. They would lock him up properly this time and he would never see his parents again! Dammit! He slammed his fist down hard on the dashboard, fighting with himself. And then, suddenly, he knew that there was only one thing that he *could* do. His parents were thousands of kilometres away and, no matter how much he wished to the contrary, quite possibly dead. Jackie Wilson, on the other hand, was close, and very much alive. It was a hard decision, but he made it. Tears welling up in his eyes, Vo Diem uncradled the microphone, and began to speak. 'Help! Help! Can anybody hear me?' he said.

A voice came back at once. 'This is VK4LB, VK4LB. Butterfly Island launch. What kind of trouble are you in?' It was Charlie.

Diem took a deep breath. 'This is Diem,' he said. 'Get the policeman. It's about Jackie. She's on the reef, with two men. I stole their boat.'

'How did you . . . ?' The static could not conceal the bewilderment in Charlie's voice. 'Never mind,' he went on. 'Give me Jackie's position. Over.'

Diem described the whereabouts of the cay as accurately as he could and then turned the cruiser around, listening to the radio as Charlie called up Bob, who was searching for Jackie from his plane. 'Diem's on his way back to the cay, Bob,' he heard Charlie say. 'It'll take me *forever* to get there in *Elizabeth*. Connolly's got boats on the way, but you'll get there first. Over.'

'Those guys might try to use Jackie as a hostage, Mr Wilson,' Bob cautioned.

'Not if we handle it my way,' Charlie crackled back. 'Listen carefully. You too, Diem.'

A three-way conversation followed, and when it ended everyone knew exactly what had to be done.

Vo Diem almost missed the cay, because by the time he returned all that was visible was a lighter, coppery-green patch on the surface of the sea, showing where it had been, and three figures; one small, two big. Through the binoculars he could see that the water was already up to Jackie's knees. She was waving. He picked up the microphone and called in. 'Nice going, Diem,' returned Charlie. 'Now move in, nice and easy. Everything depends on timing your move just right.'

Diem inched the throttle forward, easing the cruiser towards the cay. He could see Madden and Pirelli quite clearly now. They were staying close to Jackie, as expected. As he shifted into neutral, letting the vessel drift, Charlie's voice came over the radio once again. 'Remember, wait until you can see the plane.' Diem turned and scanned the sky. There it was, like a white moth, dropping down out of the blue, right on schedule!

The cruiser was very close to the cay now, and he could hear Jackie's voice, warning him to be careful. He looked across the intervening water, carefully judging the distance between the boat and the men. Close enough. He reached out and turned the key. The engines spluttered, then coughed, then died.

'He's stalled! Come on, Pirelli!' Madden called. Leaving Jackie, he began to wade out towards the boat. Pirelli paused for a couple of seconds, then followed. Diem nodded with satisfaction; so far, so good.

He looked around for the seaplane. It was on the water now, at the opposite end of the cay, taxying in wide circles, and as Diem watched, the hatch opened and Sally leaned out. 'Swim, Jackie! Swim for it!' she yelled, but Jackie was already on her way, running through the water as far as she could, then striking out and swimming for her life. As the seaplane bore down upon her it seemed for a moment that she would be run down, but Bob had judged it to perfection. Sally reached out and in one movement scooped her sister up and hauled her inside. The hatch slammed shut, the motor opened up with a roar and the machine planed across the surface, then lifted and was away.

Diem looked back towards his end of the cay. Madden and Pirelli were dangerously close now, in deep water, swimming powerfully towards him. In a few strokes Madden would be alongside. Quickly, Diem tossed a couple of life-jackets into the water, then reached forward and turned the key. The engines burbled into life, and he accelerated noisily away, leaving the two men cursing, treading water, and on their own!

Sergeant Connolly radioed Charlie later in the day, to announce that Madden and Pirelli had been picked up by a police launch. He had some other good news, too. David Lee had been intercepted at Ellis River Airport, just as he was about to board a southbound jet. He had an air ticket to London in his possession, but in the circumstances, the Sergeant didn't think he'd be going *anywhere*.

The announcement of Lee's arrest was a bonus, sparking off loud cheers as the whole family gathered in the family-room to celebrate Jackie's safe return. But Andrew injected a sour note. Standing in the centre of the room, serious-faced, he reminded them that they weren't out of the woods yet. There was still the future of Butterfly Island to consider. 'Judging by the Government survey, the oil down there is worth a lot more than one million dollars,' he said, staring hard at Charlie and gently stroking his bruised jaw. 'But you'll have to tear Butterfly apart to get at it.'

Charlie looked at the kids. 'You understand what this

means?' he asked quietly. They nodded, one by one. 'It's *your* future,' Charlie continued. 'It's up to *you*.'

Jackie spoke first. 'I want to keep the island the way it *is*,' she said, looking remarkably fit despite her recent ordeal. Charlie nodded; he'd expected as much. He looked at Greg.

'If we did the place up, gee, that's *worse* than selling out,' said his son.

All eyes were on Sally now. She hesitated for a moment, torn between two sets of hopes and desires. 'Oh, what the heck!' she sighed at last, throwing herself down into an easy chair. 'I wouldn't know *how* to be a millionaire. Leave the oil in the ground, Dad.' As Charlie's face cracked into the first broad smile they'd seen for days she raised a warning finger. 'I'm still going away,' she added,' but I want this place to come home to.'

'What do *you* think, Mary?' said Charlie.

'Well, it's nothing to do with *me*, really,' Mary replied, surprised and flattered to be asked. 'But I'm proud of the lot of you.'

Andrew paced up and down the room. 'This is just the kind of sloppy, sentimental decision that I expected this family to make.' Avoiding Charlie's gaze, he looked hard at the kids. 'I think I've got a point to prove to your father,' he went on, 'and since he's such a hard, calculating bloke, who's looking for money to invest in the future of this island, well, it had better be *my* money. That way, we'll keep it in the family.'

Charlie was dumbfounded. He moved over to his brother, amid a chorus of expressions of surprise and delight from the rest of the family. 'You're *full* of surprises today, aren't you?' he said.

Andrew nodded. 'Mind you, I expect a bigger slice of the action.'

'We'll talk about it,' said Charlie. Smiling, he held out his hand.

EPILOGUE

Cairns International Airport was a hive of activity. As well as a number of domestic jets, the tarmac contained a gaggle of light planes that were the lifelines of the isolated cattle stations and missions across the Great Dividing Range. And towering over them all was the gigantic shape of a Qantas jumbo jet.

Inside, the terminal was crowded and noisy. There were people everywhere, checking tickets, waiting for baggage, chatting with friends, but despite the activity and excitement, a friendly, casual, easy-going atmosphere prevailed, in the true tradition of the Australian North.

Three passengers waited at the Qantas Departures Desk; a man, a girl, and an Asian boy. All were neatly, but casually dressed, and carrying airline bags, and as the traffic officer handed their tickets across the counter a public address announcement echoed around the concourse. 'First and final call for passengers on Qantas Flight QF13 for Djakarta, now boarding at gate six.'

'That us!' said Charlie. He handed Jackie her ticket, then held out another one to Vo Diem. Diem looked at the brightly-coloured piece of paper and card, then at Charlie's beaming face, and then at Jackie; and for the first time ever, she saw him really smile. Slowly, almost reverently, he reached out and took it. Charlie put his arm around them both. 'Come on,' he said, 'let's go and find your Mum and Dad,' and together they walked towards the departure lounge.

If you have enjoyed this book you may like to read some more exciting BBC/Knight stories:

RICHARD COOPER

CODENAME ICARUS

'Smith: you are a dirty, messy, stupid, lying clown.'

Martin Smith's parents had been to see his Head Master. Again. The same grumbles, the same complaints, the same feeling of the sour defeat of all their hopes for the boy.

'Word is that you're thick. You know that, don't you?'
'Should do sir. I've been told often enough.'

How then does Martin Smith gain a place at Falconleigh, a school for children gifted in science and maths, and part of the mysterious Icarus Foundation? And who is the enigmatic figure behind Icarus, and what are his aims?

CLIVE DOIG

PUZZLE TRAIL

Who stole the Puzzleton Plans?

Who is the Conundrum Castle murderer?

What's been buried on Puzzle Island?

The answers to these and many other tantalising puzzles are within this exciting, sometimes exasperating, book. But first you have to outwit master puzzler Clive Doig by solving the clues on each page. And things aren't always that straightforward . . .

Based on BBC television's immensely popular PUZZLE TRAIL, this book is guaranteed to provide hours of fun, frustration and entertainment.

BBC/KNIGHT BOOKS

SID WADDELL

JOSSY'S GIANTS

Glipton Grasshoppers are rubbish! They're the pits – as boys' football teams go, they don't!

And when ex-Newcastle player Jossy Blair sees their antics on the pitch he suggests their manager would be better off running a safari park than a football team . . .

However, Tracey Gaunt, the team's bucket girl, doesn't intend watching the Grasshoppers collapse without a fight. And her first task is to persuade Jossy to take them on.

BBC/KNIGHT BOOKS

ALSO AVAILABLE FROM BBC/KNIGHT BOOKS

RICHARD COOPER
☐ 27535 9   Codename Icarus   £1.25

CLIVE DOIG
☐ 36193 X   Puzzle Trail   £1.25

SID WADDELL
☐ 38727 0   Jossy's Giants   £1.50

All these books are available at your local bookshop or newsagent, or can be ordered direct from the publisher. Just tick the titles you want and fill in the form below.

Prices and availability subject to change without notice.

KNIGHT BOOKS, P.O. Box 11, Falmouth, Cornwall.

Please send cheque or postal order, and allow the following for postage and packing:

U.K. – 55p for one book, plus 22p for the second book, and 14p for each additional book ordered up to a £1.75 maximum.

B.F.P.O. and EIRE – 55p for the first book, plus 22p for the second book, and 14p per copy for the next 17 books, 8p per book thereafter.

OTHER OVERSEAS CUSTOMERS – £1.00 for the first book, plus 25p per copy for each additional book.

Name ....

Address ....

....